Jane Austen's *Emma*

A Critical Study

Therese Burgess

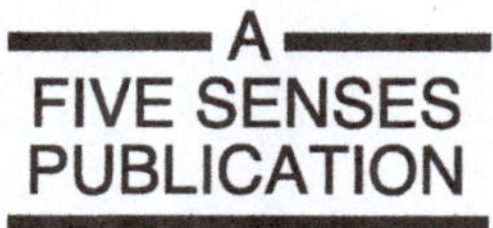

First published 2023

Five Senses Education Pty Ltd
2/195 Prospect Highway,
Seven Hills 2147
NSW Australia

Burgess, Therese
Jane Austen's *Emma* – A Critical Study
ISBN 978-1-76032-293-9

Contents

The text used in this guide is the Penguin edition of *Emma* (2015) with introduction and notes by Fiona Stafford. This is based on the first edition of the novel and retains original spellings and punctuation. As in the first edition, the novel is divided into three volumes.

- Volume I Chapters 1 to 18
- Volume II Chapters 19 to 36
- Volume III Chapters 37 to 54

How to Study a Novel

To study a novel effectively, you must be systematic. When you are reading, give your full attention to the novel.

- Read the novel *at least* twice. Your first reading can be quick, allowing you to take note of the characters, events and general tone.
- Read the novel slowly, making notes on characters, plot events, themes and language features.
- Read in blocks of *at least* half an hour. This is to prevent a fragmented view of what you are reading.
- From which point of view is the novel told? An omniscient narrator? A narrator who is one of the characters?
- If told by a narrator, is this narrator reliable?
- How do you respond to the characters? Is the narrator guiding you to respond in a particular way? Does your viewpoint change at any point in the novel?
- What narrative techniques are used?
- Are there any recurrent symbols, words or events which are significant in understanding the novel?
- Does the novel have textual integrity? Do form and language produce a unified whole?
- Is the structure of the plot linear or non-linear?
- What overall themes emerge as you read?
- Is the setting important? What are any significant features?
- Is the ending satisfactory? Does it leave any unanswered questions?

Critical Study of a Text

In a critical study of a text, your aim is to develop your own interpretation through a careful and deliberate process of reflection, discussion, and testing and refining your ideas against critical sources.

This process will necessitate a number of re-readings. It is not enough to read a complex text once. Successive re-reading will reveal more of the text's complexities to you and will allow you to strengthen your interpretation.

A critical study will obviously require a sophisticated understanding of the plot and its structure, characters, setting, themes, and language techniques and textual aspects. You will need to consider how all of these features contribute to the textual integrity of the text.

For a critical study, you must also take into account the context and the impact which this has had on the text's reception. Not merely the temporal and spatial aspects of context, but also the political, economic and sociological background of the text must be considered. All of these factors can affect the action of the plot, the behaviour of the characters and the values inherent in the text.

Once you have begun to develop your distinctive understanding, it is essential to examine some critical resources and to test and refine this interpretation against them. In this way, a considered interpretation, closely tied to the text can be developed.

The Author

Jane Austen was born on 16th December, 1775, in Steventon, Hampshire. She was the second youngest child in a family of eight children, of which six were sons, and Jane and her sister, Cassandra, the only daughters. Her father was a vicar of the Anglican Church and the family belonged to the middle class or gentry.

Jane was educated mainly at home, apart from a period at boarding school in Oxford and later Southhampton with Mrs Ann Cawley, and another short stretch at Reading Abbey Girls' School until the fees proved too high for her father's income. She was allowed free access to her father's library and that of a family friend, Warren Hastings. Her father encouraged both Jane and Cassandra to write, draw and to stage and act in plays for the family.

Austen wrote stories and poems from an early age. These early works are now referred to as *Juvenilia* and span the period, 1787–1793. Between 1793 and 1795, Austen wrote the epistolary novel, *Lady Susan* and an incomplete novel entitled *The Watsons*.

In 1801, Rev. Austen retired from his parish and moved his family to Bath. Austen was discontented in Bath and her productivity declined. After the death of Rev. Austen, the ladies of the family lived for a time with Jane's brother, Francis. Later, another brother, Edward, who had been brought up by wealthy relatives, was in a position to offer them a home in Chawton in 1809. Here, Jane recovered her creative spark.

Austen's first published novel was *Sense and Sensibility* (1811), followed by *Pride and Prejudice* (1813), *Mansfield Park* (1814) and *Emma* (1815). All of these were published anonymously. Two further novels, *Northanger Abbey* and *Persuasion* were published posthumously and under the author's name.

Austen never married, but she had relationships which proved unsatisfactory in various ways. Her friendship with Tom Lefroy, to whom she seems to have been very much attracted, was curtailed by his family because of lack of money on both sides. In 1802, she received a proposal of marriage by Harris Bigg-Wither, a long-term family friend. At first, Jane accepted as the marriage would have been advantageous financially, although there was little about the young man to recommend him. However, she quickly came to her senses and withdrew her consent.

In 1815, Austen became ill. It is not possible to know exactly what her malady was, but medical experts have speculated that it might have been either Addison's Disease or tuberculosis. Yet despite her frailty, Austen continued to write, working on *Persuasion*. During her last months, she was nursed devotedly by her sister, Cassandra. She died on 18th July, 1817.

Little of substance is known about Jane Austen's life. After her death, her brother, Henry, wrote a biographical note to preface the posthumous novels, and while this presents her as living 'a life of usefulness, literature and religion'[1], it does little to present an authentic personality. Her nephew, James Edward Austen-Leigh in *A Memoir of Jane Austen*, gives the reader the vital information that 'her needlework both plain and ornamental was excellent' and 'she was considered great in satin stitch'.[2] Austen wrote freely to her sister, but after her death, Cassandra destroyed much of the correspondence. Had she not, we might have had a more rounded idea of the author, beyond this picture of a rather prim maiden aunt who was accomplished in all the essential feminine arts. It is left to modern readers to consider her ironic observation of her society and to surmise what this woman may have been like to know.

Jane Austen never received critical acclaim for her novels during her lifetime. The public enjoyed them, and Austen kept a record of comments people had made about them.

1. Austen, Henry, 'Biographical Notice of the Author'. *Persuasion* by Jane Austen. (1965) Penguin, Hammondsworth. pp 29–34
2. Austen-Leigh, James Edward, 'A Memoir of Jane Austen'. *Persuasion* by Jane Austen. (1965) Penguin,Hammondsworth. pp 267–391

For an accessible and illuminating study of Jane Austen, look at — Lucy Worsley, *Jane Austen at Home*. (2017) London, Hodder and Staunton.

Context

During Jane Austen's lifetime there were great changes in England. The loss of the American colonies, the French Revolution and the conflict with Napoleon altered the position of England in the world. The Industrial Revolution began to have an influence on urban, but not yet rural, life. None of these events have any prominence in Austen's novels which are concerned with the lives of people in rural English villages.

Society in Georgian England was still quite rigidly stratified. At the top were the aristocracy, those with titles, ranging from knight down to baronet. They frequently lived in great houses, surrounded by parkland and they employed an army of servants to maintain all of this. A member of the aristocracy might have an income of one hundred thousand pounds a year.

Jane Austen's family belonged to the gentry which was the next level. They were relatively financially secure. The gentry kept a number of servants and possibly had a horse-drawn conveyance of some sort (tied to income per year). They were loyal subjects of the monarch, conservative in their views and were usually strong Anglicans.

Although at this time those engaged in professions and in trade were regarded by many as not quite on the same level as the gentry, those making their living in this manner were slowly gaining acceptance as the industrial revolution began to have its impact on the social order. This is illustrated by Mr Weston, whose family 'for the last two or three generations had been rising in gentility and property' (Chapter 2) and whose engagement in trade has allowed him to make his fortune, to purchase Randalls and to marry Miss Taylor.

Manual workers such as farmers were on a lower level. Emma tells Harriet when discussing the Martin family that they could not possibly mix with such people. If they were poorer, then the gentry might be 'useful' to them, as Emma advises Harriet. (Chapter 4)

This table shows what incomes per annum meant in practical terms:

25 pounds	A farm labourer, a poor curate, a shopkeeper or a governess might earn this.
100 pounds	The recipient of this income might keep a maid, but living on this would be difficult for a couple.
400 – 500 pounds	The family could have two maids and a serving man. They would not be able to afford a carriage.
700 – 1000 pounds	The family could have a carriage and would live quite comfortably if they were careful.
2000 pounds	The family would be very comfortable on this income unless they had many children and were not careful with their budget.
4000 pounds	The family would very likely have a country estate as well as a house in London.
10 000 + pounds	A member of the aristocracy or an untitled member of the highest level of the gentry might enjoy this income.

Women had few options. They looked forward to marriage and a family. Marriages were usually founded on good financial sense and a woman of good fortune had more options than one with a small one. Hopefully, the marriage would be also grounded in affection, and Austen's novels underline this. Inheritance passed to the male heirs of the family, and if the estate was entailed, property might pass to a distant cousin, as in *Pride and Prejudice*. Unmarried women without sufficient fortune were dependent on the goodwill of the male members of family. (On the death of Jane Austen's father, she and her mother and sister lived first with one brother, Frank, and his wife, and then were offered a house by another brother, Edward.) An unmarried woman might seek work as a governess. This could be a good outcome and the woman might find a congenial situation as in Miss Taylor's case. However, in Jane Fairfax's case if she had needed to take up this position, it is likely that this intelligent and accomplished young woman would have been subservient to Mrs Elton's equally crass friends.

Women generally married young. Lydia in *Pride and Prejudice* marries at sixteen, and Elinor and Marianne in *Sense and Sensibility* are married in their late teens. They usually went on to have many children and childbirth was fraught with danger. Austen had a sister-in-law who died after giving birth to her eleventh child. This era, however, saw the beginnings of feminism. Mary Wollstonecraft, in *A Vindication of the Rights of Women*, criticised the idea that women could no nothing beyond marry and procreate. A number of other women writers also debated the narrow nature of women's education.

Girls were educated differently to boys. Whereas boys might have been taught the sciences, the classics (Latin and Greek) and maths so that they might progress to university, girls were not taught any of these. They may have been instructed in history, geography, French and Italian, as well as the desirable feminine accomplishments such as music, singing, drawing and embroidery. These accomplishments were designed to demonstrate her suitability to a prospective husband and later to enhance their social life.

Women could not divorce, so were obliged to endure an unhappy or abusive marriage. Men could divorce in extreme circumstances, but the inevitable scandal would deter most from taking this course.

Behaviour and etiquette were governed by precise social conventions. There were rules for introductions and for addressing people, for making social calls, for mixing with other ranks of society.[3] Behaviour and etiquette were closely observed by all. Any breach of etiquette, such as dancing more than twice with the same partner at a ball, would be the subject of discussion and rumour. Mrs Elton breaks the rules of decorum by being boastful and rude.

Gentility and the nature of a gentleman were matters of concern to Austen's characters and to polite Regency society. A gentleman was not necessarily titled, nor a great landowner. He was one who displayed the correct behaviour and obeyed the rules of etiquette. Emma asks Harriet to consider Mr Weston and Mr Elton and 'their manner of carrying themselves; of walking; of speaking; of being silent'. (Chapter 4)

3. Read 'Jane Austen and Social Judgement' by Kathryn Sutherland on the British Library website, for more illumination on this.

The British Library website has many other articles on social class, marriage and the position of women. The website is – *www.bl.uk* > articles > jane-austen

The Novel in Austen's Day and Jane Austen's Anonymity

The novel was neither widely read nor accepted as a genre when Jane Austen was born. Conservative elements in society feared that novels would fill people's minds with dangerous ideas. Novels would make people dissatisfied if they read of lives preferable to their own. Reading novels was a waste of time which could be more productively used in other pursuits. People were warned that excessive reading of novels could even result in postural harm from remaining in one position too long or in eye-strain! The critics felt that people should confine themselves to reading biographies or sermons, works which would uplift them. However, Jane and her family read widely, including novels.

The greater use of the printing press and the growth of a middle class with money to buy books and leisure to read them, fostered the proliferation of the novel. Yet, the critics continued to air their views.

Austen touches on this tension in *Pride and Prejudice* when Elizabeth Bennet defends herself from the comment that she reads a great deal, the implication being that this was somehow trivial and time-wasting. In *Northanger Abbey*, Austen takes the deeply ironic viewpoint that reading Gothic novels leads Catherine into unfortunate behaviour!

From this, we can understand that criticism of the novel was possibly one of the reasons that Jane Austen's first novels were published anonymously. Another reason was that the society of the time did not sanction women of her class working, and writing for remuneration would have been seen as work. At the same time, Austen's patriarchal society was reluctant to recognise talent in a woman. Many other writers, at that time and later, used male pseudonyms or remained anonymous. These included the Bronte sisters, Mary Shelley and Mary Anne Evans (George Elliot).

Jane Austen's novels were only published under her own name after her death.

Synopsis of the Text

Emma, a young woman of almost twenty-one, is 'handsome, clever and rich' (Chapter 1). She is the younger of two daughters of the indulgent, widowed Mr Woodhouse and has just seen her governess / companion, Miss Taylor, marry Mr Weston and move some distance away. Emma, whom we are also informed enjoys 'too much of her own way' and thinks 'a little too well of herself' (Chapter 1), is now rather isolated. She replaces the absent Miss Taylor with Harriet Smith, a young girl of unknown parentage, whom she decides to befriend and encourage with the view of helping her make a good marriage.

Emma quickly diverts Harriet's interest away from a young farmer, Robert Martin, who is paying court to her and the girl rejects his proposal. Despite the advice of her friend and neighbour, Mr Knightley, Emma influences Harriet to think favourably of the young vicar, Mr Elton. She does all she can to foster their relationship, but is horrified when Mr Elton proposes to her instead. Harriet is very upset and Mr Elton departs for Bath, while Emma feels contrition for a time.

However, Emma soon occupies her mind with new diversions. Jane Fairfax, the young relative of the Bates ladies arrives for an extended visit. Emma is jealous of Jane who is equally beautiful, but more accomplished than Emma, and they have a cool relationship. Mr Weston's son, Frank, who has been brought up by his aunt and uncle, the Churchills, also arrives in Highbury. Frank and Jane have met previously in Weymouth. Frank is very gallant to Emma and for a time, she is sure she is in love with him. Later, she decides she isn't, but remains convinced that he is in love with her. Emma begins to think of him as a possible husband for Harriet.

Jane receives an anonymous gift of a piano and there is much speculation as to who has sent it. Frank and Emma concoct a scandalous story about the anonymous donor and Jane, and tease her about it with hints. News comes that Mr Elton has married and soon he arrives back in Highbury with his *nouveau riche* heiress who has a fortune of ten thousand pounds.

A ball is held and during the course of it, Mr Elton refuses to dance with Harriet, which is an unconscionable slight. Mr Knightley dances with her instead. Emma is delighted by his kindness. Harriet, however, starts to entertain romantic notions about him. Unwittingly, Emma encourages her, thinking that Harriet is interested in Frank Churchill.

An excursion is held to Box Hill and during the course of it, Emma is rude to Miss Bates. Later, she is castigated by Mr Knightley. Emma is devastated by the realisation of how badly she has erred and the fear that she has lost Mr Knightley's good opinion. Shortly after this, the news comes of both Mrs Churchill's death and of Frank Churchill and Jane Fairfax's secret engagement which has been in existence since Weymouth.

Emma relates the news to Harriet, expecting her to be upset, but the girl is unconcerned and reveals that it is Mr Knightley, not Frank Churchill, whom she loves. She feels that he returns her sentiments. At this point, Emma realises that she, herself, loves Mr Knightley. She is horrified at the thought of the unequal match which would be a great debasement for him. Emma wishes with all her heart that she had never begun to encourage Harriet!

Mr Knightley speaks to Emma, whom he fears is upset at Frank Churchill's engagement. Emma reassures him that her heart was never truly involved. Mr Knightley proposes and is accepted. Harriet is dispatched for a holiday in London to get over her supposedly broken heart. While there, she meets Robert Martin and he proposes again. This time, Harriet accepts. Emma is delighted as Harriet is assured of a secure future.

Mr Woodhouse's dislike of change which seems to threaten the marriage plans is circumvented by the proposal that Mr Knightley should live at Hartfield.

Chapter Summaries and Commentaries

Volume I

Chapter I (1)

The chapter begins with the introduction of the protagonist, Emma Woodhouse. We are informed that she is 'handsome, clever, and rich', one who 'seemed to unite some of the best blessings of existence', a young woman of 21 who has had a happy, untroubled life thus far.

We learn that Emma's mother died when she was young and that since that time she has had a governess, Miss Taylor, who was more friend than mentor. Emma has enjoyed the independence of running her father's household since the marriage of her older sister, Isabella. Miss Taylor has just married Mr Weston and moved a short distance away at the commencement of the narrative. Emma has mixed emotions about this event: happy on her friend's behalf, but aware of what her loss will mean. With Miss Taylor, Emma has enjoyed a friendship of unconditional acceptance and affection. The perceptive reader will realise that the narrator's purpose is to lead them to suspect that not all will regard Emma in this way and neither should they.

This chapter introduces Emma's father, Mr Woodhouse, a man limited by 'habits of gentle selfishness', and extreme hypochondria and fussiness. Although Emma cares for him with love and forbearance, he is 'no companion' for her, and not an intellectual equal. Mr Knightley, a key character, also makes his first appearance in this chapter. He shows some awareness of the changes for Emma entailed by Miss Taylor's marriage.

The setting of the novel, Highbury, is a 'large and populous village' which the Woodhouse estate of Hartfield adjoins. Mr Knightley's estate of Donwell Abbey and the Westons' establishment of Randalls are within easy walking distance of the village. Within the neighbourhood of Highbury, the Woodhouses are 'first in consequence'. Emma has no friends there with whom she can socialise on an equal basis now that Miss Taylor has moved away.

Emma believes that she has 'made the match' between Miss Taylor and Mr Weston. Although she is challenged by Mr Knightley as to her actual effectiveness in this endeavour, she asserts that 'it is the greatest amusement in the world' and determines to match-make for Mr Elton, the young vicar.

Commentary

The use of the qualified verb 'seemed' in the first sentence signals that all is not as positive as might appear at first sight. The narrative voice follows on from this by using the strong word 'evils' to inform us that Emma has had 'rather too much her own way' and that she has too high an opinion of herself. A little further on, 'evil' is again used to describe Emma's lack of suitable companionship and her danger of 'suffering from intellectual solitude' now that Miss Taylor has married. The reader is positioned to expect that these factors will likely coalesce with unfortunate consequences.

When we learn that Emma believes that she has had success in match-making and intends to continue with this 'amusement', we suspect that the consequences will be interesting.

Chapter II (2)

In this chapter, we learn the history of Mr Weston. He had been a captain of the militia when he first married, but this had been a disastrous union, both personally and financially. When his wife died, of an unspecified 'lingering illness', leaving him with the care of a small child, he resolved upon 'a complete change of life'. The child, Frank, was relinquished to his maternal aunt and uncle, the Churchills, and Captain Weston 'quitted the militia and engaged in trade'. He was sufficiently successful in his endeavours in this quarter to be able, after more than twenty years, to buy a small estate and to marry again.

Frank became the Churchills' heir and assumed their name when he came of age. Mr Weston saw him, once a year in London and 'was proud of him'. It is now expected that Frank will visit his father and new mother. He has written Mrs Weston 'a handsome letter', about which there has been much discussion in Highbury, and the visit is anticipated with keen interest.

Commentary

Mr Weston's history offers insights into the attitudes and structures of society in early 19th century England. Although Miss Churchill's marriage does not threaten the finances of the 'family-estate' in any way, it is deemed 'an unsuitable connection' as Captain Weston has no fortune. Thus the marriage results in her estrangement from her family.

However, Mr Weston has later been able to improve his financial situation and his social status by his successful career in trade. He has risen in 'gentility and property'. This points to the gradually changing social attitude towards trade.

We learn that Highbury is prepared, on his father's word, to accept Frank Churchill as 'a fine young man' and to be keenly interested in him. The reader is led to wonder if, when he does come, the reality will match the expectation.

Chapter III (3)

Mr Woodhouse enjoys the company of his friends and thus Emma usually organises them either to dine or to play cards most evenings of the week. The guests are the Westons, Mr Knightley and Mr Elton, the young vicar. There is also 'a second set'; those lower socially, yet perfectly acceptable. This set comprises Mrs and Miss Bates, who are a vicar's elderly widow and her middle-aged, unmarried daughter. As well, there is Mrs Goddard who runs a small boarding-school.

Mrs Goddard requests to be allowed to bring a Miss Smith with her to one of these evening get-togethers. Harriet, now seventeen, is 'the natural daughter of somebody' and has been at the school for several years. Emma is very interested in Harriet and resolves to not only 'continue the acquaintance', but to 'improve' Harriet, encouraging her away from her present friends and introducing her to another level of society. Harriet is gratified by the attention of 'so great a personage' as Emma.

Commentary

This chapter introduces both Harriet Smith and Emma's plans regarding her. Emma reveals herself to be rather snobbish, arrogant and self-deceiving. She makes assumptions about the suitability of Harriet's friends without knowing them and congratulates herself on her plan regarding Harriet.

Emma is quite delighted with her plan, telling herself it is 'a kind undertaking' and one 'highly becoming' to her. The repetition of the verb 'would' in Emma's musings reflects her confidence that her course of action is appropriate and will be achieved. The plan will not only be 'kind', but will be a 'becoming' one which will no doubt bring Emma praise. The subtext is that Emma wants to be well thought of in her circle. Harriet is quite dazzled by Emma's attention and will be a willing subject.

There is humour in the description of Mr Woodhouse's attempts to control what and how much his guests eat. Emma manages the situation by allowing him to fuss, while quietly providing for them.

Chapter IV (4)

Emma and Harriet begin to spend a great deal of time together. Harriet has spent time at Abbey Farm with the Martins and when Emma discovers that Mr Martin is the unmarried son, she suspects 'danger'. She warns Harriet of the dangers of being acquainted with his wife, when he does marry, as she will be a 'mere farmer's wife'. Further, Emma is concerned that Harriet herself may be attracted to Robert Martin. When they meet him on the road, the excited Harriet seeks approval of him from Emma, but instead hears extreme criticism that belittles the young man.

Emma takes the opportunity of extolling the virtues of Mr Elton, who is the young man she intends for Harriet.

Commentary

We see Emma's self-described 'kind designs' being put into action. She sabotages Harriet's interest in Robert Martin by describing him in strongly negative terms and comparing him unfavourably with the 'gentlemen' in Emma's circle. The reader cannot help but perceive Emma herself in a negative way. Her choice of words to describe Robert – 'clownish', 'a very inferior creature' and 'illiterate and coarse' - borders on vicious. Emma shows herself to be a snob here as she is far too aware of her own social status and has pretensions to being better than those below her.

Chapter V (5)

Mr Knightley and Mrs Weston disagree on the merits of Emma's association with Harriet. While Mrs Weston is delighted that Emma has a female friend, Mr Knightley feels that Harriet's 'delightful inferiority' will enhance Emma's good opinion of herself. Mrs Weston persuades him not to share his reservations with John and Isabella when they come at Christmas, as he will upset Emma's sister who is 'easily alarmed'.

Commentary

This chapter lays down some further foundations on which the plot will be built. The possible future difficulties Frank Churchill will cause are foreshadowed in Mrs Weston's comment: 'No, Mr Knightley, do not foretel vexation from that quarter.'

Mr Knightley unwittingly reveals his attraction to and interest in Emma. He confesses that he has 'seldom seen a face or figure more pleasing to me', but justifies his statement by saying he is just 'a partial old friend'. He has 'a very sincere interest' in her, but it is a brotherly interest. Mr Knightley disguises his feelings about Emma, even to himself. He wishes to see her in love and 'in doubt of a return'. This foreshadows another development in the plot. Mr Knightley sees Emma as having some growing up to do, wondering 'what will become of her', a rather negative sentiment. It seems that the Westons entertain hopes of a match between Emma and Frank.

Chapter VI (6)

Emma's matchmaking continues. She decides to paint Harriet's portrait and enlists Mr Elton's help in accomplishing this. He constantly compliments Emma's talent and reputes any criticism. When the portrait is finished, he volunteers to take it to London to be framed.

Commentary

The narrative voice reveals that Emma has a more realistic view of her talents than she wishes other people to have. When the portrait is finished, she knows its shortcomings, but will not admit them. Mr Elton is very ready to contradict any criticism of it.

Emma demonstrates her ability to interpret anything Mr Elton says and does as motivated by interest in Harriet. His admiration is for Emma's artistic skill, not for the subject of the portrait. The irony of the last paragraph is that she comes close to discerning the realities of the situation, but her focus on her match-making will not allow this to happen.

Chapter VII (7)

Harriet receives a letter containing a marriage proposal from Robert Martin. Emma is very surprised on reading the letter to find that it is composed well and executed with 'no grammatical errors'. Harriet asks for direction from

Emma who then conducts a masterly manipulative campaign to ensure Harriet does not give a favourable answer. While telling Harriet that she 'will have nothing to do with it', she confuses Harriet and finally succeeds in pushing her to refuse Mr Martin. The letter of refusal is written and 'though Emma continued to protest against any assistance being wanted, it was in fact given in the formation of every sentence'. Then, she diverts Harriet from any feelings of regret about her action by speaking of Mr Elton and how he is doubtless showing her picture to his mother and sisters.

Commentary

The words 'a fresh occasion for Emma's services to her friend' do not prepare the reader for what the services actually entail! Harriet is delighted to receive the proposal and clearly hopes that Emma will approve of the letter. She is no match for the wily Emma who skilfully pushes for the result she wants – a refusal. She uses her claims of friendship and of being older to sway Harriet, stirring up a whirlpool of doubt and confusion in the naïve young girl and all the time protesting that she does not want to 'influence' her! Finally, when Harriet has decided on refusal, Emma uses emotional blackmail to deliver the coup de grace. She says, 'I could not have visited Mrs Robert Martin, of Abbey-Mill Farm. Now I am secure of you forever.' While marvelling at Emma's manipulative skills here, the reader feels sympathy for poor Harriet, and fears what the outcome may be for her. Does Emma really know what she is doing?

Chapter VIII (8)

Emma resolves to keep Harriet at Hartfield. Mr Knightley visits and reveals that he knows of Robert Martin's feelings toward Harriet and that he believes the match would be a good one. Emma discloses the rejected proposal. They argue and part in mutual vexation. Afterwards, Emma is 'frightened' to recall his opinion that Mr Elton will only make a financially judicious match, but convinces herself that she knows best. Her self-deception is reinforced by relayed gossip from Miss Nash. It seems that Mr Elton is interested in a lady and to Emma's mind, whom could that be except Harriet?

Commentary

The word 'safest' reveal that Emma wishes to keep Harriet away from any possible meeting with Robert Martin. It is certainly 'safest' for the successful execution of Emma's schemes, but as Mr Knightley's sentiments reveal, not necessarily so for Harriet's future good.

Mr Knightley sees the advantages of the match with Robert Martin for Harriet. His only scruples in advising Robert Martin to propose are that the match might be 'beneath' him due to Harriet's uncertain parentage and because she has little to recommend her beyond being pretty and 'good-tempered'. He accuses Emma of giving Harriet 'a sense of superiority' and advancing her unrealistic expectations. Emma, because she has decided in her own mind that Harriet must be a gentleman's daughter, perceives the girl as belonging to a higher social class than she actually does. Previously, Mr Knightley has expressed the worry that Emma's influence will 'put her out of conceit with all the other places she belongs to'. It seems that he was right and these new ideas with which Emma has filled Harriet's head may be disastrous for her future.

The force of Mr Knightley's anger is demonstrated by the words, 'nonsense, errant nonsense', the verb 'cried' and the abrupt way in which he leaves that is at variance with his usual decorum.

Chapter IX (9)

Harriet is involved in making a collection of riddles, copying them into a booklet which she is ornamenting prettily. Emma asks Mr Elton to write one for them. He brings one which he says is by his friend, but Emma believes that he has written it himself and moreover, that it is a proof of his intentions towards Harriet. Although Emma is now certain that Mr Elton is preparing to propose, she cautions Harriet to behave with decorum until this actually happens.

Emma and her father discuss the forthcoming visit by Isabella and John Knightley and their children.

Commentary

When Mr Elton visits, his attention is primarily on Emma. It is her name which springs first from his lips and he addresses her rather than Harriet. Emma, firmly in her happy schemes, sees him as being diffident around Harriet because of his feelings. She actually finds his posturing a little ridiculous.

Chapter X (10)

Emma and Harriet make a visit to a poor family. As they walk, Emma expresses the idea that she will never marry and that she will be very content in the single state. After the visit, they meet Mr Elton. Emma continually contrives to allow Harriet and Mr Elton to walk together. She is disappointed that he does not disclose his feelings to Harriet.

Commentary

This chapter reveals one of the duties that were incumbent on someone of Emma's position in society, namely visiting the poor and offering whatever help was deemed appropriate by the conventions of the time. This help appears to consist in 'comfort and advice' and a pitcher of broth from Hartfield.

Emma and Harriet's discussion on unmarried women reveals how wealth and class changed society's perception of an unmarried woman. Emma tells Harriet that 'a single woman, of good fortune, is always respectable, and may be as sensible and pleasant as anybody else'. However, 'a single woman, with a very narrow income, must be a ridiculous, disagreeable, old maid'. Wealth creates this gulf. The conversation turns to Jane Fairfax, of whom Emma seems jealous. Jane's uncertain marriage prospects and the distinct possibility of her being 'an old maid' will be an important issue later in the novel.

Emma is sufficiently confident of Mr Elton's intentions towards Harriet to say when they see his house, 'There go you and your riddle-book one of these days'. Her machinations to allow them time to walk and talk together provide humour in this chapter. Emma's belief that he 'will hazard nothing till he believes himself secure' will shortly prove deeply ironic.

Chapter XI (11)

John and Isabella Knightley with their many children arrive from London to spend Christmas at Hartfield. Mrs Weston's move to Randalls is discussed and Frank Churchill's failure to visit is raised.

Commentary

This chapter briefly outlines the personalities of Isabella and John, and shows more of Mr Woodhouse's 'peculiarities'. We learn that John is sometimes irritated into giving Mr Woodhouse a 'sharp retort'. Mr Woodhouse's self-absorption provides humour as when he describes Miss Taylor's happy marriage as 'a grievous business' and bemoans the fact that she has to go home to her husband after visiting them!

Chapter XII (12)

Mr Knightley is invited to dinner, the first occasion Emma has seen him since their quarrel over Harriet's proposal. They talk, and Emma discovers that Robert Martin has been deeply disappointed for which she expresses sorrow and they shake hands, reconciled as friends again.

Commentary

The discussion on sea-bathing shows how tedious Mr Woodhouse can be, and also how diplomatically and lovingly his daughters deal with him. There is humour in the way that Emma, Isabella and Mr Knightley attempt fruitlessly to steer the conversation away from Mr Woodhouse's preoccupations.

Chapter XIII (13)

A dinner party at Randalls is planned for Christmas Eve. Harriet develops a sore throat and returns to Mrs Goddard to be nursed there. When Emma meets Mr Elton she attempts to dissuade him from going to Randalls as well, but John Knightley offers a place in his carriage. Emma is disconcerted that Mr Elton still wishes to go when Harriet will not be there. John Knightley suggests to Emma that she is the object of Mr Elton's interest, and that she should be circumspect in her manner towards him. She is astonished and is quite sure her brother-in-law is wrong.

Commentary

Yet again, Emma tries to control the interactions of Harriet and Mr Elton. She attempts to keep him from the party at Randalls as she hopes he will then sit anxiously at home, 'sending to inquire after Harriet every hour of the evening'. His obvious delight at the thought of the dinner she rationalises away as that of a young man who enjoys going out. In the carriage she is disconcerted as Harriet seems to have been forgotten 'in the expectation of a pleasant party'.

There is wonderful irony in Emma's 'consideration of the blunders which often arise from a partial knowledge of the circumstances'. Emma is thinking of John Knightley's observation, but the astute reader will see that this is directed at Emma herself. She will fall into this trap a number of times before she learns discretion.

Chapter XIV (14)

Emma resolves to put Mr Elton's unsatisfactory behaviour out of her mind, but is sorry to find that he is seated close to her at the dinner table, and intent on monopolising her attention. She is 'very cross' at missing interesting conversation because of this, but outwardly remains well-mannered.

The subject of Frank Churchill is raised and Emma muses that she has a predisposition to think well of him.

Commentary

Mr Elton's excessive attentions cause Emma to give some credence to the idea that he may be interested in her, something she feels is 'absurd and insufferable'. She wonders if he has transferred his feelings from Harriet to her.

The vagaries of Enscombe are discussed first by Mr Weston and then by Mrs Weston. The reader wonders how much Mrs Churchill's wishes restrict Frank's movements and how much he uses them as a convenient excuse.

Chapter XV (15)

Mr Elton continues his surprising behaviour, first seating himself between Mrs Weston and Emma, and then assuming the 'right of first interest in her' to urge her to avoid going to see Harriet. Emma is extremely upset by this.

The news that it is snowing breaks up the party and in the confusion of leaving, Emma finds herself alone in one of the carriages with Mr Elton. Almost immediately, Mr Elton astonishes and discomforts Emma by professing his love of her and expecting a favourable response from her. Emma speaks of his 'attentions' to Harriet and he declares that he never thought of her except as Emma's friend. It is obvious that he believes himself to be Emma's equal and that he perceives Harriet to be very much his inferior. He accuses Emma as having given him 'encouragement'. Emma rebuffs him, saying that she has only ever seen him as her friend's admirer. They part in mutual anger and poor Emma has to compose herself, determined to reveal nothing of her inner turmoil to her family.

Commentary

Mr Elton has done exactly what Mr Knightley predicted he would do. He has attempted to connect himself well. He couches his proposal in extreme language. He will 'die' if she refuses him and he feels 'unequalled love and unexampled passion'. Obviously, he feels that marriage to Emma would be 'an equal alliance' and is aghast at the thought of, in his view, a grossly unequal marriage to Harriet. His conceit and lack of genuine feeling are clear to the reader from the studied words and phrases of the proposal, devoid of any genuine feeling.

Chapter XVI (16)

Emma mulls over the events of the evening. She now realises that Mr Elton is proud and conceited, and has always been determined to make a good match with someone of fortune.

Emma examines her own behaviour and has to admit that it might have been construed as encouragement by Mr Elton. She realises that Harriet will suffer when she learns what has happened. She is profoundly distressed by this unwelcome turn of events.

Commentary

We do feel sorry for Emma in the aftermath of Mr Elton's proposal. Up until now we have been amused by her machinations. She had been annoyed that John Knightley saw her as 'blind', yet in fact she has been just this. The revelation has been deeply painful for her. She castigates herself as 'having blundered most dreadfully' and resolves 'to do such things no more'. The reader's sympathies are engaged by her obvious distress, but at the same time there is some doubt as to whether her contrition will have lasting effects.

Mr Elton has also been 'blind'. He has been keenly aware that Harriet was below him in social status, yet he is unaware that he is equally below Emma.

Chapter XVII (17)

Mr Elton goes to Bath for a few weeks. Emma has told Harriet of Mr Elton's proposal. Although Emma had consoled herself that Harriet would not be upset for long as her feelings were not 'acute and retentive', the girl grieves painfully. Emma knows that she must help Harriet to recover by showing her attention and affection.

Commentary

Mr Elton's letter to Mr Woodhouse announcing his removal to Bath pointedly excludes Emma. This is intentional and it is also extremely rude. He reveals clearly that his charming manners are all on the surface and there is no real gentility of manner underneath.

In the aftermath of Mr Elton's proposal, Emma had consoled herself by rather condescendingly thinking that neither he nor Harriet had any deep feelings, and thus would not suffer from this debacle. However, she is obliged to admit that Harriet has been 'more resolutely in love' than she had perceived. Because Harriet's sufferings are due to Emma's meddling, she is clear-sighted enough to realise that she must help the girl to recover her equanimity.

Chapter XVIII (18)

Frank Churchill has not arrived for the proposed visit. Emma and Mr Knightley discuss him. They disagree and Mr Knightley becomes quite angry. Emma cannot understand why.

Commentary

Mr Knightley perceives Frank Churchill to be 'proud, luxurious, and selfish', a superficial young man who spends his time in 'some watering hole or other'. When speaking of him, he uses 'ought' frequently, conveying that Frank is failing in his duty. He sees Mrs Weston as being slighted by Frank's failure to come. He believes that Frank uses his letter writing skill to manipulate situations to his advantage. Mr Knightley senses that Frank is charming but insincere.

Emma is more positive about Frank and wonders if he has a 'mild' personality which would make dealing with conflict difficult. No doubt, her own family experiences make her aware that a person cannot always speak or act as they might wish.

What is the source of Mr Knightley's 'vexation'? Is he jealous of Emma's positive interest in Frank? Or is he annoyed that Emma champions someone that he feels he cannot respect?

Reflect on these questions:

- What benefits are there for Emma from her friendship with Harriet?
- Find examples of Emma's lack of awareness of Mr Elton's true intentions.
- Has Emma learnt her lesson?
- Mr Knightley always seems able to maintain an open-minded and reasonable approach to people and events. Why might he show 'a degree of vexation' in his discussion of Frank Churchill with Emma?

Volume II

Chapter I (19)

Emma is out walking with Harriet. She decides to call on Mrs and Miss Bates to divert Harriet from thoughts of Mr Elton. She feels that she will be safe from having to listen to much rereading and discussion of any letter from Jane Fairfax because it is not her time to write to her relatives. However, Jane has written an unexpected letter telling of her plans to visit for three months. Emma has to listen to a recount of the arrival of the letter and the circumstances of its being written, but manages to escape before the actual letter is read out to her.

Commentary

We learn how much Emma dislikes visiting the Bates, a 'deficiency' in the duties to be expected from one of her station in Highbury. In contrast, the ladies are kind and hospitable. Emma is apparently impeccably polite, expressing interest in the letter, but the reader will not miss the irony in 'I was afraid there could be little chance of my hearing anything of Miss Fairfax today' and guessing at her suppressed irritation. She entertains scurrilous fantasies about Jane and Mr Dixon and questions Miss Bates about Jane's reasons for coming, hoping to find evidence for them.

This chapter shows Miss Bates' extreme garrulousness. The length of her speeches and the need to include every detail and thought reveal both her great affection for and interest in Jane. We can also appreciate how tedious she could quickly become!

Postage was expensive at this time. This is why Jane would only write at certain intervals and why Emma did not expect that the Bates would have had a letter from her.

Chapter II (20)

Jane Fairfax is an orphan, the only child of Mrs Bates' youngest daughter. Both her parents died young and after a short time with Mrs and Miss Bates, Jane was taken to live with Colonel Campbell who had known and admired Lieut. Fairfax, her father. She has been given 'excellent education' — at least in the terms of the day. Although 'beloved' by the Campbells, they are not in a position to bestow any fortune on her and she will need to seek employment as a governess. The likelihood of her making a good marriage in financial terms is very slight.

Jane comes for the promised visit and spends an evening at Hartfield.

Commentary

Emma's feelings about Jane are always in a state of flux. She moves from 'dislike' to admiration to 'compassion and respect' to irritation again. Jane's unwillingness to gossip about the Dixons or about Frank Churchill whom she has met in Weymouth provokes Emma.

This chapter contains a comment by the narrator that though Jane's explanation about not accompanying the Campbells to Ireland is a truthful one, 'there might be some truths not told'. It is a fleeting note of mystery for the perceptive reader.

Chapter III (21)

Mr Knightley visits and comments favourably on Emma's manner towards Jane the evening before. However, they quickly disagree on whether Jane is 'reserved' or 'diffident'. Emma has sent a hind-quarter of pork to the Bates, and they and Jane appear to thank the Woodhouses. Miss Bates conveys the news that Mr Elton is to be married, to a Miss Hawkins.

Emma is concerned about the effect of this news on Harriet who is still extremely interested in Mr Elton. At this point, Harriet rushes in and announces that she has spoken to Robert Martin and his sister. Harriet burbles on about the meeting, until Emma, to put the subject out of her mind, tells her about Mr Elton's engagement.

Commentary

There are a number of undercurrents in this chapter. We learn that Mr Knightley disapproves of Emma's want of friendliness towards Jane Fairfax, and is happy when Emma seems to be making an effort to be more gracious.

As well, it seems that Mr Elton's interest in her has not been as secret as Emma had hoped. Mr Knightley indicates by a smile that he suspects it and Mrs Coles has hitherto suggested it to Miss Bates.

Emma persists in her delusions about the unsuitability of a connection for Harriet with the Martins. She concedes that they 'well meaning, worthy people' but still ascribes their desire for the match to a wish for the family 'to rise' socially. Given that Harriet's heritage still remains unknown, this is a misguided idea. Emma, however, is not as comfortable with her position on the Martins as she had been.

Chapter IV (22)

In Highbury, there is great speculation about the intended Mrs Elton and without anyone yet meeting the lady, she is judged to be 'handsome, elegant, highly accomplished, and perfectly amiable'. A very self-satisfied Mr Elton returns briefly to Highbury. Emma wonders how she could ever have thought him 'pleasing at all'.

Harriet is invited to Abbey Mill Farm and Emma reluctantly decides that the girl must go, albeit for a very short visit.

Commentary

Emma is happy to discover that although Miss Hawkins has ten thousand a year, she has no connections to gentility and is the daughter of a merchant. In Emma's mind, she is not 'Harriet's superior'. Emma finds that she is still dealing with the effects of her aborted match-making for Harriet who is still feeling pain.

Chapter V (23)

Harriet makes a short visit to Abbey Mill Farm. The Westons expect an imminent visit from Frank. However, he comes a day early and visits Hartfield with his father. Emma finds him an 'agreeable' young man. As he leaves, he indicates that he will call on the Bates and Jane Fairfax, whom he is 'acquainted with' from Weymouth.

Commentary

Emma knows that Harriet's very short visit to the Martins has caused both her and the family some pain. However, she convinces herself, yet again, that all of her actions in that sphere have been correct.

When Frank visits, Emma is aware that Mr Weston has hopes that she and Frank might form an alliance. She wonders if Frank is thinking along the same lines.

Chapter VI (24)

Frank, Mrs Weston and Emma walk about Highbury. When he sees the Crown Inn, he wonders why balls are no longer held there. He is very keen to see the practice restored. They visit Ford's where he buys some gloves. They discuss Jane Fairfax and Frank criticises her pale complexation and reserved nature. He suggests that in Weymouth, Mr Dixon may have been more interested in Jane than in Miss Campbell.

Commentary

We see here that Frank begins his devious game. The words with which he describes her appearance, 'a most deplorable want of complexion' and her reserve, 'a most repulsive quality' are very strong and intended to convey that he has absolutely no interest in her. To leave no doubt at all, he says, 'One cannot love a reserved person'. He is evasive about how much he saw her at Weymouth, side-stepping the question by exclaiming over Ford's. When Emma is invited to pose the question gain, he gives an answer that is no answer at all, and when further pressed, he says they were all 'in the same set'. It suits his purposes very well to suggest something inappropriate between Mr Dixon and Jane.

Emma' imagination, meanwhile, is running away as usual, believing when Frank discusses Mr Elton's small house that he is amenable to the idea of settling down in a small establishment.

Chapter VII (25)

Frank Churchill rides to London to have his hair cut, occasioning sharp criticism from Mr Knightley who comments he is 'just the trifling, silly fellow I took him for'. The Coles invite Emma and her father to dinner and after some demurring as they are on a lower social level, Emma accepts.

Commentary

Emma has decided that she would like the attention from 'all their joint acquaintance' which would result from Frank Churchill falling in love with her. Accordingly, she is able to talk herself out of the misgiving she has on learning of his London jaunt.

The rest of the chapter describes Emma's feelings about a dinner invitation from the Coles who are 'of low origin' and 'only moderately genteel'. From initially believing that they should not 'presume' to invite the 'best families' and that she should teach them a lesson by declining the invitation, Emma is irritated when she is not invited at all. When eventually, an invitation comes, she changes her mind and accepts. From this we can see that the strict conventions of Regency society are gradually being loosened.

Mr Knightley reveals again by his scornful comment that he does not hold Frank in any high regard.

Chapter VIII (26)

At the Coles' dinner party, the news is shared of a pianoforte having been delivered to Jane Fairfax, the day before. It has been suggested that it was a gift from Col. Campbell. Frank and Emma discuss the gift. Emma first of all hints to him that the gift may have come from Jane's friend, Mrs Dixon, and then settles on Mr Dixon. She has concocted in her own mind a scandalous relationship between Mr Dixon and Jane Fairfax.

Emma is very satisfied with the attentions Frank is paying her and quite sure that 'everyone must perceive it'. Mrs Weston, though, discomforts Emma by suggesting that Mr Knightley could be attracted to Jane Fairfax.

Commentary

Emma is concerned with appearances. She is very happy to see that Mr Knightley has come in his carriage, 'as became the owner of Donwell Abbey'. In fact, he has brought his carriage so that he might offer transport to Miss Bates and Jane Fairfax. His impulse has been kindness, not prestige, and reveals the inner worth of the gentleman, not his concern with appearing to be a gentleman.

Frank Churchill continues his devious game. He is very happy to allow Emma to share her suspicions about the pianoforte. He states that 'I can see it in no other light than as an offering of love'. This will prove ironic as the plot further unfolds. Emma catches him staring intently at Jane and he passes it off by commenting on Jane's odd hairstyle. Later, he compares Jane's dancing very unfavourably with Emma's. Emma is very happy to see all of this as proof that Frank is becoming attached to her.

Emma's reaction to Mrs Weston's suggestion about Jane and Mr Knightley is quite strong. She calls it 'a very shameful and degrading connection'. Her ostensible reason for her dislike of the idea is that little Henry would lose his inheritance. Perhaps there are underlying feelings of which Emma is as yet unaware?

There is wonderful irony in Emma's comment to Mrs Weston that she takes up an idea and runs away with it! Emma has not yet learned to refrain from doing this herself.

Chapter IX (27)

Emma is very pleased in retrospect with her visit to the Coles. Yet, she has a stirring of conscience about sharing her suspicions about the pianoforte with Frank Churchill. Harriet has had news of Robert Martin and Emma judges it wise to keep her close, lest there be any accidental meetings with him. She meets Mrs Weston and Frank and they all visit the Bates.

Commentary

This is a richly comic chapter. It begins with Emma's great degree of satisfaction that the Coles must have been delighted with her presence at dinner. Her self-satisfaction is extreme and the Coles are viewed as 'worthy people' who deserve to be happy.

The chapter continues with the description of Harriet in Ford's and is a parody of an indecisive shopper. Equally, Miss Bates' dialogue is a parody of a well-meaning, but garrulous speaker. It is no wonder that Jane Austen's contemporary readers delighted in her comic characters.

Chapter X (28)

Frank begins to tease Jane about the pianoforte and continues on to make references to Weymouth and to Irish melodies. Emma is uncomfortable with his comments. Mr Knightley is spied from the window and Miss Bates has a loud conversation with him to which the others listen. He is on the point of coming in, but on learning that Frank Churchill is there, he declines.

Commentary

This chapter appears to give Mrs Weston more evidence for her suspicions about Mr Knightley and Jane Fairfax. Not only has he been very generous in his provision of apples, leaving his own household short, but he is solicitous about her health.

Chapter XI (29)

Frank and Emma discuss the possibility of staging a ball. Randalls is considered and rejected. The Crowne Inn is next discussed, with many objections based on its being 'damp and dangerous' raised by Mr Woodhouse. However, the Crowne is selected and Frank writes to Enscomb to propose an extension of his stay.

Commentary

Emma has some slight misgivings about Frank Churchill's manner, but as she reminds herself, she does not intend to marry him, and brushes them aside. Mr and Mrs Weston are gratified that Frank has secured the first two dances at the ball with Emma.

Chapter XII (30)

Mr Knightley is not impressed with the plans for the ball. He says he will come and attempt to 'keep as much awake' as he can. Frank Churchill receives a letter, summoning him to Enscomb because Mrs Churchill is ill. The plans for the ball are postponed indefinitely.

Commentary

When he is about to take his leave of Emma, Frank Churchill seems about to make a declaration of some sort. Emma believes he intends to propose and diverts him. Later in the novel, this incident will be referred to and explained.

When he leaves, Emma decides that her feelings of 'listlessness, weariness, stupidity, this disinclination to sit down and employ myself, this feeling of everything's being dull and insipid about the house' must be proof that she is 'a little in love' with him. The reader can see that she is toying with the idea of being in love as a diversion.

At the same time, Jane Fairfax is 'particularly unwell' for a time. Later, the reader will realise that this is the effect of stress and uncertainty about her future.

Chapter XIII (31)

Emma amuses herself by fantasizing about the progress of a relationship with Frank Churchill, one which concludes with her refusing him. Frank, she imagines, with her usual egotism, as being very much in love with her. A letter from Frank to Mrs Weston mentions Harriet and she wonders if perhaps her friend might replace her in his feelings. Then she checks her speculations in a half-hearted way.

News of Mr Elton's impending wedding keeps Harriet 'anxious and restless'. Eventually, Emma speaks quite sternly to her and Harriet grieves over her ungratefulness.

Commentary

Emma's botched matchmaking continues to cause difficulties for Harriet. Yet, Emma allows herself to speculate on Harriet's superiority over Jane Fairfax, and to muse on a possible attachment with Frank Churchill.

Chapter XIV(32)

The Eltons return to Highbury and a number of visits ensue so that all might meet the bride. Harriet is very impressed with Mrs Elton, but Emma reserves judgement until the second visit has occurred.

Commentary

In this chapter, Mrs Elton's conversation produces the same feelings in the reader as it produces in Emma. Mrs Elton is an 'insufferable woman'. She admires Hartfield, only in that it resembles Maple Grove. She does not realise that it offends decorum to compare houses. She talks endlessly about herself, her tastes and habits. Condescendingly, she offers to introduce Emma into Bath society. She is astonished that Mrs Weston, although having been Emma's governess, is 'really quite the gentlewoman' and that 'Knightley' is 'quite the gentleman'! Again, her presumption in referring to Mr Knightley by such a familiar name offends decorum.

Emma is delighted that Mr Elton has married such an appalling woman. She comments that Mrs Elton is 'much beyond my hopes'. Mr Woodhouse, with his usual lack of perspicacity, finds her 'a very obliging, pretty-behaved young lady'.

Chapter XV (33)

Emma shows no wish to become friends with Mrs Elton. Although the Eltons feel dislike of both Emma and Harriet, they dare not show disrespect to Miss Woodhouse. Instead, they behave contemptuously toward Harriet. Mrs Elton decides that she will pay her attentions to Jane Fairfax and surprisingly Jane does not rebuff her. Emma challenges Mr Knightley on the 'extent of his admiration' for Jane Fairfax. He acknowledges that he considers Jane 'a very charming young woman', but says that he would want 'an open temper' in a wife. Mrs Weston is still not convinced.

Commentary

We see how superficial and unpleasant the Eltons are. They vent their ill-will at Emma's failure to embrace Mrs Elton as a social equal, on the harmless Harriet, a simple young girl.

Emma's overactive imagination seeks reasons for Jane Fairfax's continued stay in Highbury. She is puzzled by Jane's acceptance of the Eltons' company, but both Mrs Weston and Mr Knightley offer thoughtful answers for why she might do this.

Chapter XVI (34)

The Eltons receive many invitations. Mrs Elton plans a 'very superior party' at which she will show Highbury 'how every thing ought to be arranged'. Emma realises that she, too, must have a dinner for them. During the course of the evening, Jane Fairfax's walks to the post office are discussed. Mrs Elton is determined that her servant will fetch Jane's letters for her, but Jane demurs. Emma is curious as to why Jane has been so adamant about fetching her own letters.

Commentary

Mrs Elton intends to set herself up as the arbiter of decorum in Highbury, clearly in opposition to Emma. She will set the standard by the ostentatious party she will have with 'more waiters engaged'. At the Woodhouses' dinner, Mrs Elton wears pearls, associated with aristocratic status, as a way to assert her idea of her own superiority in Highbury circles. However, every time she speaks, she reveals her ignorance and presumption.

Mr Knightley is caustic about Frank Churchill's writing, saying that 'it is like a woman's writing'. Is he provoked by Emma's admiration for Frank's hand?

Emma notices that Jane has 'a glow', and attributes it to the receipt of a letter.

Chapter XVII (35)

Mrs Elton is determined to assist Jane Fairfax in obtaining a situation as a governess. Jane is equally determined not to make any enquiries, but to enjoy the next few months in Highbury. Mr Weston arrives with a letter from his son, with news of the Churchills' move to town (London) and the likelihood that he will be able to visit more often.

Commentary

Mrs Elton's unsubtle attempts to push Jane Fairfax into obtaining a post 'in the first circle' make the reader cringe. Yet, Jane is gracious in refusing to be coerced into acting before she is ready, revealing her dignity. Mrs Elton likes Jane because she is on a lower social plane and Mrs Elton can be seen to be doing charitable services for her. Yet, we know from her earlier comments about Mrs Weston that she does not believe governesses can have any gentility. This puts the charity of the intentions into doubt.

Mrs Elton again makes us cringe when she refers in an overfamiliar way to Mr Woodhouse as 'this dear old beau of mine' and gushes about his 'quaint, old-fashioned politeness'. There is comic relief in Mrs Elton's monologue about her dress, when she claims that her 'natural taste is all for simplicity' and almost in the next breath, considers putting trimming on a simple gown.

Chapter XVIII (36)

Mr Weston talks of Frank to Mrs Elton. The difficult and dominating personality of Mrs Churchill is also discussed.

Commentary

In this chapter, Mr Weston's description of Mrs Churchill who has 'no pretence of family or blood' and who is 'an upstart' is juxtaposed with the sentiments of Mrs Elton, an upstart. She relates her 'horror of upstarts', and yet again, attempts to claim gentility by association with the Sucklings and Maple Grove. There are multiple layers of irony here.

Reflect on these questions:

1. Compare Mrs Elton's feelings about the Tupmans in this chapter with Emma's opinion of the Coles in Chapter 25. Are they equally snobbish? Does Austen wish the reader to perceive Emma differently to Mrs Elton?
2. How is Mrs Elton's attempt to interfere in Jane's life different to Emma's constant intrusion in Harriet's?

Volume III

Chapter I (37)

Frank Churchill returns to Highbury and visits Emma. Mrs Churchill finds London not suitable for her delicate constitution because of its noise and the family moves to Richmond. Both Frank and Mr Weston are delighted by this turn of events as Frank will be more easily able to visit. The ball at the Crowne is once again planned.

Commentary

Emma examines her feelings and concludes that she is no longer in love with Frank. However, she is concerned that he may not feel the same and is apprehensive about his making 'an absolute declaration'. When she meets him, he seems 'less in love', but very restless and hurries away after a quarter of an hour. Emma, in her wonderful egotism, ascribes this to 'a dread of her returning power'! It does not occur to her that his haste might have any other reason for it.

Chapter II (38)

The ball is held. Emma observes Mr Knightley and wishes he would dance. Mr Elton slights Harriet by refusing to dance with her. The Eltons maliciously exchange 'smiles of high glee'. Mr Knightley observes the slight and gallantly partners Harriet instead. Emma and Mr Knightley discuss the event and then dance the last dance together.

Commentary

Emma is annoyed that having been asked to come early to the ball to see that all is as it should be with the rooms, she discovers that many other people have also been asked by Mr Weston to come early for the same purpose. Later, she has to submit to Mrs Elton, being the new bride, opening the ball which Emma 'had always considered … as peculiarly for her'. Despite these two annoyances, she enjoys herself. She observes Mr Knightley and decides 'there was not one among a whole row of young men who could be compared with him'. At the same time, Mr Knightley seems often to be observing her. Neither of them are aware of their deepest feelings towards each other. After the Eltons' appalling behaviour, they talk and although she admits that she did want Harriet to marry Mr Elton, he does not censure her and praises Harriet, expressing the opinion that it would have been a better match.

Frank's restlessness is again in evidence at the beginning of the ball. He is clearly waiting for someone to come, but Emma believes it is just that he wants to ball to begin.

Chapter III (39)

Emma indulges in happy recollections of the ball. She is happy to have come to a position of understanding with Mr Knightley regarding the Eltons, and Harriet. The incident at the ball will finally lay to rest Harriet's infatuation.

Harriet is harassed by gypsies and Frank Churchill rescues her. Mr Woodhouse is extremely anxious about the event.

Emma is incorrigible! She begins to imagine an attachment between Harriet and Frank Churchill. She tells herself that she will not act, but simply wish for this to happen.

Meanwhile, Frank Churchill's subterfuges continue. He uses the excuse of the scissors to call on the Bates.

Chapter IV (40)

Harriet brings out a box of 'treasures' she has kept. They are a plaster that Mr Elton touched and his cast-off pencil. She proposes now to burn them. She announces that she will never marry because the object of her affections, is too far superior to her, for her ever to have hopes.

Commentary

At Harriet's mention of a person 'so superior to Mr Elton', Emma immediately jumps to the conclusion that she is interested in Frank Churchill. Harriet says that she does not have 'the presumption' to expect a return of her feelings. She cautions Harriet to be careful, and to observe the person's behaviour before revealing any feelings. Then, she goes on to bolster Harriet's hopes by saying that 'more wonderful things have taken place, there have been matches of greater disparity'! Emma is pleased at the thought of this attachment for Harriet, believing it will 'raise and refine her mind'.

Chapter V (41)

Mr Knightley observes the interaction between Frank Churchill and Jane Fairfax, and wonders if there is 'something of private liking, of private understanding even'. Frank and Emma play a game with letters, and upset Jane. Knightley discusses the supposed relationship with Emma, who states confidently that there is no attachment between them.

Commentary

Frank slips up when he mentions Perry's carriage and tries to pass it of as something he dreamed. Mr Knightley observes all of this, hoping to find grounds for his suspicions about Frank and Jane Fairfax. He observes the game with letters and feels that 'it was a child's play, chosen to conceal a deeper game on Frank's part'. Quite sure of Frank's deviousness now, he decides to warn Emma, whom he fears has feelings for Frank. But, when he speaks to Emma, her confidence that his suspicions are groundless coupled with her animated mood, discomforts him and he leaves rapidly, 'too much irritated for talking'.

We wonder what the grounds are for Mr Knightley's extreme reaction. Is it hurt pride at being accused of letting his imagination run away? Is it annoyance that Emma seems to know Frank Churchill's mind? Or is it suspicion that Frank may be trifling with the affections of two women?

Chapter VI (42)

An excursion to Box Hill is proposed, but postponed. Instead, Donwell Abbey and its strawberries is chosen as a substitute. Mrs Elton continues to pressure Jane Fairfax to allow her to facilitate a situation for her. Jane leaves early. Frank Churchill does not come until late and is in a bad temper.

Commentary

There are a multitude of undercurrents in this chapter with many people preserving the appearance of decorum, while irritations, anxieties and animosities swirl under the surface.

Emma is again annoyed at 'the unmanageable good-will of Mr Weston's temper'. Her excursion to Box Hill with her own select group, has been sabotaged by being united with Mrs Elton's party, and although she is outwardly courteous in agreement, inwardly she seethes.

Jane Fairfax seems almost at breaking point as her outburst to Emma reveals. The reader suspects that the cause of Frank Churchill's ill-humour has to be more than just the heat.

There is much humour in the interchange between Mrs Elton and Mr Knightley; the overbearing lady attempting to take over as the hostess, while he politely but firmly resists all her suggestions. Mrs Elton seems to see herself as part of some romantic idyll, drifting about in a big hat with a basket over her arm, while all admire her!

Chapter VII (43)

The Box Hill party occurs on the day after the Donwell Abbey excursion, but it does not go well. There is 'a want of spirits, a want of unison'. Frank and Emma flirt with each other. Frank tells the group that Emma wants everyone to say 'one thing very clever…two things moderately clever…or three things very dull indeed'. Emma insults Miss Bates by telling her she is limited to 'only three'. Miss Bates is hurt and Mr Knightley upbraids Emma for her unfeeling remarks. Emma is profoundly upset by his criticism.

Commentary

This chapter is a pivotal one in the novel. Frank and Emma flirt out of boredom, or perhaps a desire to evoke some response from their glum companions. Emma reveals her vanity by imagining how their behaviour would be described in letters written by Mrs Elton and Jane Fairfax. Later, we will discover how painful this thoughtless behaviour has been to Mr Knightley and to Jane.

When Emma is criticised by Mr Knightley, she first of all dismisses her words as what anyone might have said, excusing herself. Then, she claims that Miss Bates did not understand the barb. Finally, she places the blame on Miss Bates' nature, in which 'what is good and what is ridiculous are most unfortunately blended'. However, as Mr Knightley points out the compassion Miss Bates is due because of her lowly situation in comparison to Emma's, his words strike her heart. She sees her behaviour exactly as it is – egotistical, cruel and demeaning to both the victim and the culprit. This incident is a crucial one in the growth of Emma's self-knowledge.

In this chapter, the undercurrents between Jane and Frank swirl ominously. There is a short interchange about the infelicity of commitments based on short acquaintance. Only later does the reader learn that there has been a serious quarrel between them the day before.

Chapter VIII (44)

Emma's conscience bothers her all evening and the next morning she visits the Bates. While there she discovers that Jane Fairfax has suddenly decided to take the situation which Mrs Elton has been foisting on her. She is to depart within a fortnight. However, at the moment, Jane is sick and Emma does not see her. Frank Churchill has returned to Richmond.

Commentary

Emma has been obliged to listen to her own conscience and to realise that her behaviour to Miss Bates has always been lacking. She has often been 'remiss' in fulfilling the obligations of her superior status to the Bates; she has, in fact, been 'scornful, ungracious'. Emma has embarked on the path of greater self-knowledge and is keenly aware that she needs to make amends.

Jane Fairfax's sudden capitulation to Mrs Elton seems inexplicable to Emma, but the reader will make connections between Frank Churchill's sudden return to Richmond and Jane's unexpected agreement to the situation.

Chapter IX (45)

Mr Knightley announces a trip to London. He is pleased that Emma has been to visit the Bates. The following day news comes of Mrs Churchill's sudden death. Emma believes this will lay the way clear for a match between Frank and Harriet.

Jane Fairfax is still ill. Emma attempts to see her and to offer comforts, but is rebuffed. Jane is seen wandering in the meadows at the same time she was supposedly too ill to drive with Emma.

Commentary

Even though Emma's attempts to help Jane have been rejected, Emma does not succumb to the vexed feelings she would once have entertained. She is 'sorry, very sorry' and feels pity for the state Jane is in. She knows that her own intentions were good and is confident that Mr Knightley would have approved of them. Clearly, his good opinion is paramount with Emma.

Chapter X (46)

Emma is summoned to Randalls where Mrs Weston tells her that Jane Fairfax and Frank Churchill are engaged; in fact, have been secretly so for some months. She assures them that she had no hopes of an attachment with Frank herself. Emma is appalled at Frank's duplicity.

Commentary

Emma has a very strong reaction to the news. Frank has revealed himself to be deceitful and to have played everyone who believed in him for a fool. The description she gives of what 'a man should be' is her opinion of Mr Knightley!

However, Emma is far more inclined to excuse Jane Fairfax's part in the scheme as she is aware that Jane needs to avert joining 'the governess trade' by finding something in the marriage market. She says with genuine understanding and compassion, 'If a woman can ever be excused for thinking only of herself, it is in a situation like Jane Fairfax's'. Emma is developing more empathy.

Chapter XI (47)

Emma is concerned how Harriet will receive the news of the engagement. She protests that she never thought of Frank Churchill. It is Mr Knightley with whom she is in love, and she believes that he returns her affection. Emma is devastated by this news. She has a blinding moment of realisation: 'It darted through her, with the speed of an arrow, that Mr Knightley must marry no one but herself'.

Commentary

Emma is confronted in this chapter with the consequences of her 'vanity' and 'blindness'. Not only has she been unaware of the promptings of her own heart, but she set Harriet on a path that may ensure this heart is left bereft. Harriet has followed her advice to be discreet, and her observations of Mr Knightley's behaviour towards her seem to prove an interest in her. Emma is obliged to concede that Harriet is not deceived as she has observed the same behaviour. Gallingly for Emma, Harriet tells her that she should never have presumed to think of him without Emma's encouragement. Emma has successfully moulded and raised Harriet from a nervous little girl, grateful for the attention of the great Miss Woodhouse, to one who has 'notions of self-consequence'. Emma has achieved the project she embarked on. Now, she must face the consequences.

Not only is her own imprudent conduct brought before her, but also 'her own heart'. She understands that she has never been in love with Frank and equally that she had been unaware of what was in her own heart.

Emma is appalled at the social degradation a marriage to Harriet would mean for Mr Knightley. She concedes that such a union is not impossible. In a short time, Emma has been forced to see herself as cruel and unthinking (Box Hill), to find that her perceptions are flawed (Frank Churchill) and to realise that her meddling has 'done mischief' (Harriet and Mr Knightley). Emma is learning many painful lessons.

Chapter XII (48)

Emma forlornly considers the changes that Harriet's marriage to Mr Knightley will inevitably cause. Mrs Weston visits Jane Fairfax, who reveals the distress the secret engagement has caused her.

Commentary

The painful revelations continue for Emma. Now that she is faced with its loss, Emma understands how she took her position in Mr Knightley's 'interest and affection' for granted.

Mrs Weston acts out of great kindness in visiting Jane and allowing her to open her heart to her. She is heartened by the sentiments communicated by Jane. Jane says she has acted 'contrary to all my sense of right' and does not deserve 'the fortunate turn that every thing has taken', nor the kindness she is receiving from the Westons, and her grandmother and aunt. Both Emma and Mrs Weston feel a great deal of sympathy for Jane.

Emma reflects further on the shabby way she has treated Jane in the past. In her former headstrong way, she ignored Mr Knightley's advice on associating more closely with Jane, allowing her jealousy to govern her feelings and actions.

Emma's emotions are turbulent and her only consolation is 'in the resolution of her own better conduct'. At this point in the novel, the reader is more confident that her contrition is genuine.

Chapter XIII (49)

Emma meets Mr Knightley. He is worried that she will be upset at the news of the secret engagement, but she reassures him that her affections were not engaged by Frank. She is in trepidation that he will disclose his love of Harriet, and stops him from speaking. Then she realises that she cannot give him pain by refusing to accept his confidence. Emboldened, he declares his love of her and she accepts.

Commentary

Mr Knightley is pessimistic about the future of the marriage between Frank and Jane. We can share his fears. A young man so dependent on attention and expecting to charm all he meets is not likely to be a settled, faithful husband.

Poor Emma is in great fear that Mr Knightley will declare his love of Harriet. Initially, she attempts to avoid the anguish she knows she will feel by stopping him from speaking. But she 'could not bear to give him pain'. His good is paramount in her thoughts, not her own. No matter what the cost to her, she will listen. He declares his feelings haltingly. He does not have the charming manners of Frank Churchill, but his feelings speak eloquently. The narrator is circumspect on what Emma says in response to Mr Knightley's declaration of love. It is left to the reader's imagination.

Chapter XIV (50)

Emma ponders the effect her attachment to Mr Knightley will have on her father and decides that while he lives, they must not marry. She is concerned about Harriet's reception of the news of her engagement and decides to write to her, rather than telling her in person. A letter comes from Randalls. It is Frank Churchill's long letter of explanation for his conduct sent to Mrs Weston.

Commentary

Frank Churchill's letter is intended to secure forgiveness from the Westons and from Emma. It is clear from the beginning of the letter that he fully expects forgiveness. 'But I have been forgiven by one who had still more to resent,' he writes and the implication is clear that others should likewise forgive him. He explains that he believed Emma suspected how matters were between Jane and himself, and that he had almost confessed the whole truth to her. Thus, he exonerates himself from any wrong-doing. In fact, he shifts the emphasis to Emma who 'never gave me the idea of a young woman likely to be attached'.

He admits that his unpleasantness to Jane was 'highly blamable' and agrees that he 'behaved shamefully'. However, Jane has now had her 'just displeasure' persuaded away and he is optimistic that 'no moment's uneasiness can ever occur between us again'.

Although the letter contains nothing of genuine remorse, Mrs Weston is pleased with it and obviously feels that it excuses Frank from any further censure.

Chapter XV (51)

Emma is inclined to take a genial view of Frank's subterfuges, but Mr Knightley is not. He reads the letter carefully, occasionally making negative comments aloud.

Mr Knightley proposes that he should come to live at Hartfield, thus allowing Emma to care for her father for the remainder of his life.

Commentary

Mr Knightley's analysis of Frank's letter reveals its moral slipperiness. Frank has always acted in his own best interests and is little aware of the real cost of his actions for other people. For Mr Knightley, Frank's duplicity serves to emphasise how important 'truth and sincerity' is for a relationship.

Emma reveals increased insight into her own motives. She had previously been concerned for little Henry's inheritance. She now realises that this was out of 'violent dislike' at the thought of a possible marriage between Mr Knightley and Jane Fairfax.

Chapter XVI (52)

Emma arranges for Harriet to stay in London with John and Isabella, in order to have her tooth attended to at the dentist. The real reason is that she does not wish to have Harriet's company just yet. She also postpones telling her father about the impending marriage. She visits Jane Fairfax and they arrive at a position of warm friendliness.

Commentary

The humour in this chapter is provided by Mrs Elton's heavy-handed attempts to convey to Emma the impression that she knows something that Emma does not. The irony is in the fact that Emma would have known of the engagement before she did.

Chapter XVII (53)

Mrs Weston gives birth to a daughter. Emma tells Mr Woodhouse of the marriage plans. As Emma expected, he is not reconciled quickly to the idea, but gentle and constant pressure from Emma, Mr Knightley, Mrs Weston and Isabella brings him to the position that it would not be 'so very bad' if the marriage took place 'in another year or two'! The news passes around Highbury quickly.

Commentary

The Eltons again provide entertainment for the reader. Mr Elton hopes that 'the young lady's pride would now be contented'. Obviously, it had been Emma's pride which had led her to refuse him. His own misplaced pride he does not own. Mrs Elton bemoans the match, and declares that Emma has inveigled him into it in some way, as she does not believe he could be in love. Her use of 'Knightley' continues to claim an equality with him which does not exist.

Chapter XVIII (54)

Mr Knightley brings the surprising news that Robert Martin has proposed to Harriet and has been accepted. He fears that Emma will be upset, but she is delighted.

Emma and Mr Woodhouse visit the Westons, and Frank and Jane are there. There is initial awkwardness, but this is soon set aside.

Commentary

This chapter explains Mr Knightley's previous interest in Harriet, which she had misconstrued as evidence of growing affection. Emma had also accepted that this was the case. He had been aware that Robert Martin was still in love with Harriet, and because of this, he determined to get to know her better. The consequence of their conversations was that he formed a very favourable impression of her.

Emma shows perspicacity when she tells Frank that he had 'very great amusement in tricking us all'. Although he denies it strenuously, the reader cannot help but agree with her.

Chapter XIX (55)

Conversation with Harriet on her return convinces Emma that love for Robert Martin has completely replaced all thoughts of Mr Knightley. Her parentage is known at last. She is the daughter of a tradesman. She and Robert are married. Harriet and Emma's friendship dwindles as time goes on.

Mr Woodhouse is distressed at the thought of a wedding occurring sooner rather than later. However, the robbing of Mrs Weston's chicken house persuades him that having the protection of a son-in-law in the house might be a very good idea.

Commentary

The wedding's simplicity displays a triumph of substance over appearance. Mrs Elton, predictably, decries the want of enough 'white satin' and 'lace veils', but Emma and Mr Knightley have no need to impress.

Reflect on these questions:

1. In what ways are Emma and Mr Knightley well matched?
2. Do you think that Frank and Jane will have a good marriage?
3. Why do you think Jane Austen has allowed Mrs Elton to have the last dialogue in the novel?
4. Given what you know of the society of the day, how do you think Mr Knightley's move to Hartfield would be perceived?

Characters

Emma

Jane Austen famously said of Emma that she had created a heroine 'no one but myself will much like'. (1) This of course, has not happened. The character presented in the first chapters of the novel is a complex one. She is snobbish, self-absorbed and determined to follow her own way despite good advice from someone she respects. At the same time, she is a loving and patient daughter, good-natured, kind to her friends and full of good intentions.

Emma has had little direction while growing up. Miss Taylor has been more of a friend than a mentor and has been, and continues to be, indulgent towards her. Her father is a hypochondriac and extremely anxious, and is much like a child in need of coaxing and comforting. He has never given her any guidance and sees her as perfect.

Emma lives in a very small world. Due to her father's anxieties, she has never been to London or to any of the places mentioned by other characters: Weymouth, Bath or even South End. She is insular in her outlook, circumscribed by the restrictions of her environment.

Mr Knightley says that 'Emma is spoiled by being the cleverest in her family'. (Chapter 5) She has a lively mind and uses it to scheme and plot with dire results. She is full of confidence and debates with Mr Knightley on an equal basis. She feels herself to be his equal and comments, 'We always say what we like to each other'. (Chapter 1)

Emma believes that she is a great observer, but she is deluded on this score. Her own self-deception and wish to perceive matters as they suit her leads to disastrous results. Her desire to mould Harriet and to detach her from what she sees as an inappropriate alliance could well have ruined the girl's chances of making any good marriage.

Emma likes to be observed. We are told that she is 'never indifferent to the credit of doing everything well and attentively'. (Chapter 3) At Box Hill, she is aware that her flirting with Frank is being observed and amuses herself imagining what Mrs Elton and Jane might write on the subject in their letters.

Emma likes to be superior. She is very conscious of her social position in Highbury and is quite scathing about the Coles who seem to be getting above themselves, even though their prosperity has permitted them to rise until they are 'second only to the family at Hartfield'. (Chapter 25) She feels she will be the appropriate person to teach them a lesson if they presume to ask the Woodhouses to dinner. Emma's need to be superior is fostered by Harriet with her lovely deference to all of her mentor's advice. Jane Fairfax challenges Emma's need to be superior. Jane is so much more accomplished than Emma. Emma cannot criticise any of her talents so she has to criticise her reserve. Emma takes delight in all Frank's nasty comments and insinuations because they belittle Jane and put her on a lower plane to Emma, who is basking in the glow of his attentions. Emma is remiss in her treatment of Jane Fairfax. She does not like Jane and Mr Knightley correctly ascribes this to jealousy. Emma eventually realises that this is, in fact, true.

At the ball, Mr Knightley talks to Emma of her 'vain spirit' and her 'serious spirit' and is sure that if one leads her wrong, the other tells her of it. (Chapter 38) This is not true early in the novel. Her 'vain spirit' leads her wrong when she belittles the worthy young Robert Martin to Harriet and encourages her to refuse him. This 'vain spirit' is responsible for disastrously trying to promote a match between Harriet and Mr Elton. All the pain occasioned by the failure of this plan is due to Emma's 'vain spirit'. But, at this point the 'serious spirit' speaks to her very plainly. We are told that 'she was quite concerned and ashamed, and resolved to do such things no more'. But, while she does not actively promote another match for Harriet, her 'vain spirit' allows her to influence Harriet when the girl appears to be in love again and to tell her that 'more wonderful things have taken place, there have been matches of greater disparity'. Her misperception tells her that the object of Harriet's affections is Frank Churchill, and of course, she is wrong. Emma's 'serious spirit' triumphs over her 'vain spirit' in the aftermath of Box Hill, when her conscience is truly engaged. The epiphany she undergoes when Harriet confesses her love of Mr Knightley furthers this process of self-awareness. 'How inconsiderate, how irrational, how unfeeling had been her conduct! What blindness, what madness, had led her on!' (Chapter 47)

Emma's 'vain spirit' has also allowed her to accept Frank Churchill's attentions as proof of love. She is delighted that other people are observing them and speculating. Later, she confesses to Mr Knightley that her vanity was flattered and she allowed him to persist when she might more wisely have told him to desist. In the aftermath of the announcement of the engagement, she realises that he had imposed on her, using her for his own purposes.

Emma can be distinctly unlikeable at times. Yet, the reader does not lose sympathy with Emma through all her arrogant meddling in Harriet's affairs, because she reports on her own experience and lays open her feelings. She can feel contrition and although her purpose of amendment does not always persist, she moves slowly towards greater self-knowledge. Emma's good qualities are frequently alluded to – her kindness, her wit and her agreeable personality. All of these factors ensure that the reader remains interested in and sympathetic towards Emma.

Mr Knightley

George Knightley is kind, thoughtful, forbearing, generous and usually right in his judgements. The name 'Knightley' can be seen as a comment on his integrity and chivalry. Harriet is a damsel in distress at the ball when Elton refuses to dance with her, and Mr Knightley rescues her from embarrassment. He is little concerned with appearances. Emma thinks that he does not use his carriage as often as a gentleman should and is delighted when he arrives in it at the Coles' dinner party. Later, she discovers that he had used the carriage to bring and take home the Bates ladies. His motivation had been generosity, not display. Another example of his generosity is the large quantity of apples which he sends to the Bates; so many that his cook is annoyed that there would not be 'another apple tart this spring'. (Chapter 27) Great care and thoughtfulness is shown by Mr Knightley when Mr Woodhouse visits Donwell Abbey. A comfortable room, heated by a fire is prepared for him, and everything that might take his interest, 'books of engravings, drawers of medals, cameos, corals, shells, and every other family collection within his cabinets' has been arranged for him to look at. (Chapter 42)

Mr Knightley is a good master of his lands and tenants. We learn in Chapter 12 that he shares 'the plan of a drain, the felling of a tree, and the destination of every acre for wheat, turnips, or spring corn' with his brother John. The impression the reader gains of the Donwell estate is that it is well run.

Mr Knightley shows no snobbishness towards people lower in station than himself. Robert Martin considers Mr Knightley 'one of his best friends' and comes to him for advice. (Chapter 8)

Mr Knightley is able to see Emma's faults and to chide her on them. Emma always receives complete approval from her father, Mrs Weston, Harriet and even the Bates ladies, so this is a necessary check on her vanity. This is often done mildly as when he advises her to let Elton make his own match. However, he reacts very strongly to the news that Emma has meddled between Harriet and Robert Martin. He labels her aspirations for Harriet 'nonsense' and he is very 'vexed' with her. (Chapter 8) Of course, he is absolutely right in his summation of the situation and if Emma had listened to him at this point, she would have saved herself and Harriet much heartache. His criticisms of Emma's behaviour at Box Hill are strong, but true. He accuses her of being 'unfeeling' and 'insolent', wanting in compassion and that she has humbled Miss Bates in company. (Chapter 43) His words are crucial in awakening Emma's conscience which she has been conveniently able to ignore on other occasions. This incident marks the beginning of her growth in self-awareness.

Mr Knightley feels great antipathy towards Frank Churchill. This begins when Frank's visit is only spoken of and he has not yet appeared in person. He is critical of Frank's failing to visit and feels that he is a 'weak young man' who is failing to do his duty. It is clear to Mr Knightley at this early stage that Emma is very favourably disposed towards Frank Churchill before he even appears. When Frank does come, Mr Knightley's jealousy of him blossoms as he observes Frank and Emma together. He is in love with Emma, but has no insight into his feelings.

Mr Knightley is fallible and at times jealousy clouds his judgement. He seems incapable of finding any good in Frank Churchill. He retains his negative feelings up to and beyond his own proposal to Emma. The best he can say of Frank at the end is that he believes that under the influence of Jane, Frank's character will improve.

Harriet Smith

When Harriet first comes to Hartfield, she is dazzled by Miss Woodhouse who is so kind to her and who seems so wise. She is very young, innocent and trusting. Thus, she is vulnerable to Emma's influence. As Emma directs her towards Mr Elton, Harriet allows her feelings to become involved and when she discovers that he has been interested in Emma not in her, she suffers pain.

As time goes on, Harriet grows in confidence because Emma gives her permission to. Emma realises that she has given Harriet 'notions of self-consequence' and that 'if Harriet, from being humble, were grown vain, it was her doing too'. (Chapter 47) These ideas of self-consequence lead Harriet to imagine that a marriage to Mr Knightley is not out of her reach.

When Mr Knightley discovers that Harriet has refused Robert Martin, he describes her derogatively as 'not a sensible girl, nor a girl of any information'. He concedes that 'she is pretty, and she is good tempered', but has no other good qualities to her advantage. (Chapter 8) However, much later, after he has danced with her at the ball, he declares that she has 'some first-rate qualities' and 'an unpretending, single-minded, artless' girl who is much superior to Mrs Elton, and by implication would have been a better match for him. (Chapter 38) He is, of course, delighted when she finally accepts Robert Martin.

Frank Churchill

The character of Frank Churchill is presented through his words and behaviour, through his letters and through the perceptions of others. The reader knows nothing of his inner thoughts.

Frank's first name is ironically assigned by Austen. Although he seems outwardly open and frank, he is actually devious and calculating. His forming of a secret engagement shows lack of integrity.

Frank 'uses' Emma in two ways. He pays court to her, thus taking attention away from any connection with Jane. At the same time, he seizes on Emma's dislike of Jane and stokes it, inviting her to join him in belittling Jane, both in private and to her face. He is very glib, always quick with an excuse or explanation for his actions. When Emma catches him staring intently at

Jane from across the room, as a lover might do, he immediately comments negatively about the way Jane has done her hair.

Frank conveys his reasons for the secret engagement in a letter, not face-to-face with the Westons. He has a talent for writing charming letters which will secure just the result he desires, and this letter is no exception.

Frank declares that he did Emma no harm with his attention, because he was 'convinced of her indifference'. (Chapter 50) He believes that she had detected the relationship with Jane and thus never took him seriously. It is very convenient for Frank to believe this because it exonerates him from his appalling behaviour. Mr Knightley objects that Frank has a mind full of intrigue, so he expects other people's minds to be the same.

Jane Fairfax

As in the case of Frank Churchill, we know of Jane only through her words and behaviour and through the perceptions of others. Her actual thoughts and feelings are hidden behind her frequently mentioned 'reserve'.

Jane has an uncertain future. Although she is beautiful and accomplished, she has no fortune. She is caught between the hope of making a good marriage and the possibility of becoming a governess. Jane makes an analogy between the slave-trade and the 'governess-trade', revealing her deep antipathy to this occupation. (Chapter 35) Mrs Elton attempts to push her into applying for a position, but she resists until she despairs of the relationship with Frank Churchill progressing to a good conclusion.

Jane gives away hints to the secret alliance when her daily trips to the post office are revealed. She quickly becomes very assertive when Mrs Elton tries to insist on her servant doing this for Jane, and then abruptly changes the subject. Emma realises the importance of the letters, yet wrongly ascribes the authorship of them to Mr Dixon.

Both Jane Fairfax and Frank Churchill act contrary to the unwritten rules of the community where everything is open and shared freely through conversation or gossip. Jane is persuaded into the secret alliance against her own conscience and suffers greatly during the course of it. Her illness after breaking off the engagement is both the reaction of her overwrought mind and body, and an attempt to escape what has become an intolerable situation. When all is revealed, and the relationship between the lovers rescued, Jane becomes relaxed, happy and far more open to Emma.

Emma has mixed feelings towards Jane. She vacillates between envy and admiration. Mr Knightley tells her that she sees in Jane 'the really accomplished young woman which she wanted to be thought herself' and while Emma denies this, there are times when her conscience suggests that it is so. (Chapter 20) After the revelation of the secret engagement, Emma is prepared to overlook the wrongness of Jane's actions as she understands what led her to enter into it. 'If a woman can ever be excused for thinking only of herself, it is in a situation like Jane Fairfax's,' she declares. (Chapter 46)

It is reasonable to fear that Jane Fairfax's marriage is likely to be less than satisfactory. Frank Churchill is self-centred, shallow and cruel, and is likely to remain so.

Mr Woodhouse

Is he just an annoying old busybody? Not according to the narrator. He has genuine concern for his friends' health, even though he always labours the point! One cannot doubt the goodness of his heart, even when he prevents his guests from enjoying food they greatly desire. However, he is gently tyrannical in his resistance to change.

Emma does not receive any paternal guidance from her father. She receives constant and complete approval from him. This has given her an unreal sense of her own superiority. Mr Knightley often plays the part of father / mentor because her father does not perceive when she has been unwise.

Some of Emma's most endearing qualities are the love and patience with which she cares for his physical comfort and his emotional well-being. She has to manage his anxieties by avoiding issues or steering conversations away from problematical areas. He is not as clever as Emma and she takes care to moderate her words if he is becoming confused.

Mr Elton

Mr Elton, the young clergyman, is 'a very pretty young man' according to Mr Knightley. (Chapter 1) In the village, he is regarded as a charming and handsome young man, who is always welcome at the dinner table. Emma perceives Mr Elton as not having any well-connected family background so he is a suitable match for Harriet. Mr Knightley attempts to tell Emma that Mr Elton means to marry well, but, after initial qualms, she dismisses the idea in favour of her own impressions.

Emma finds Mr Elton's studied charm only tolerable in so far as she sees it intended for Harriet. In fact, 'there was a sort of parade in his speeches which was very apt to incline her to laugh'. (Chapter 9) She frequently issues invitations to Hartfield to further her matchmaking plans for Harriet. These overtures and Emma's friendly manner with him, are construed by Elton as encouragement and proof of a growing attachment to him. He is shocked when she rebuffs him. But even worse, by telling him that she intended him for Harriet, she insults him. She suggests his social inferiority and he never forgives her for this.

As a clergyman, one would expect that Mr Elton has certain obligations of behaviour to fulfil. However, he transgresses these by his rudeness to Harriet, a young and vulnerable girl, at the ball. After this incident, Emma tells Mr Knightley that 'there is a littleness in him which you discovered, and I did not'. (Chapter 38) Emma was deceived by appearances.

Mr Elton manages to connect himself well to an heiress, but he marries a pretentious and socially gauche woman whose vulgarity he cannot perceive. He has raised himself financially, but he has not raised himself socially. Ironically, he is proud of his inelegant and social climbing wife.

Mrs Elton

Mrs Elton is a member of the *nouveau riche*, a pejorative term for the 'newly rich', people who have recently acquired money which has allowed upward social mobility and conspicuous consumption. They lack the background and education to behave well. Mr Elton has married Miss Augusta Hawkins rapidly because she has wealth but she is the daughter of a merchant. Mrs Elton constantly tries to overcome her relatively lowly origins by referring to her sister who has married well and boasting of 'spacious apartments' and 'two carriages'. (Chapter 32)

Mrs Elton hopes to equal or even outshine Emma in the social circles of Highbury. When she first visits Hartfield, she frequently compares it with Maple Grove, her brother-in-law's estate, suggesting by this that she and the Woodhouses are on a similar social level. She patronises Emma by offering to arrange introductions for her in Bath and tries to enlist Emma in setting up a musical club. When Emma does not take up her suggestions with delight, she becomes distant, and expresses her dislike of Emma by being unkind to Harriet.

Mrs Elton in her arrogance thinks that she can improve Highbury society. She plans to hold 'one very superior party', with extra waiters, and this will show Highbury society how entertaining should be done. (Chapter 34) At the dinner Emma is obliged by social expectations to hold for the Eltons at Hartfield, Mrs Elton wears pearls. Pearls have a long association with royalty and aristocracy, and by wearing them, she is signalling that she feels she is at the top of the social hierarchy.

Mrs Elton is so unaware of social conventions that she does not realise when she has overstepped them. She refers familiarly to Mr Knightley as 'Knightley' and finds him to be 'quite the gentleman', and she is astonished that Mrs Weston, a former governess is 'quite the gentlewoman'. (Chapter 32) At the Hartfield dinner, she calls Mr Woodhouse, 'this dear old beau of mine'! (Chapter 35) She is quite unaware that she is committing social faux pas and is obnoxious in her pretensions.

In one respect, Mrs Elton and Emma can be compared. Both meddle in the affairs of others. Emma interferes in Harriet's life, steering her away from Robert Martin and towards Mr Elton, Frank Churchill and, inadvertently, Mr Knightley. Mrs Elton pushes Jane Fairfax towards a position as a governess. Emma is motivated by a genuine wish to see Harriet make a good match. She is misguided, but well-intentioned. However, we surmise that Mrs Elton looks down on governesses, given her surprise at how genteel Mrs Weston is. Why then is she so keen to see Jane established as a governess? Is it genuine concern for Jane's uncertain future? Or does she wish for the satisfaction of achieving a result, very much like Emma's satisfaction when she believed she made the match between the Westons?

Mrs Weston

Mrs Weston (Miss Taylor) has been Emma's governess for sixteen years and the relationship between them has evolved over time into 'the intimacy of sisters'. She is a gentle, mild natured woman who loves Emma dearly and continues to be interested in her life and is always ready to spare time for her.

Mrs Weston rises socially through her marriage. She is prepared to love her step-son and entertains hopes of a match between Emma and Frank. When the secret engagement becomes public, Mrs Weston is anxious that Emma's affections might have been engaged wrongly by the young man.

Mrs Weston is very kind to Jane Fairfax in the aftermath of the revelations. She takes Jane for a drive, allowing her to share the difficulties and anguish of the past months. Mrs Weston shows the empathy to Jane that characterises all her interactions.

Mr Weston

Mr Weston is good-natured man, very open in all his dealings and in this way, the opposite of his son, Frank. He believes the best of everyone, constantly excusing Frank for not visiting when he should, and regarding Mrs Elton as just a pleasant young bride.

Emma feels that Mr Weston's goodwill is too expansive! She is annoyed when she finds that she is not the only person invited early to the ball, to review the arrangements. She thinks 'a little less of open-heartedness would have made him a higher character', but this reveals more about her than about him. (Chapter 38) He is, however, a dreadful gossip.

The Bates

Mrs and Miss Bates are a pair of ladies who have lost all their wealth. They behave with gentility and are welcome in the social circle of Highbury. Both the Woodhouses and Mr Knightley are kind and generous to them as they realise how difficult poverty now makes their lives. Miss Bates is full of good-will, but extremely garrulous. Austen presents Miss Bates' monologues in full. This is wonderfully comic, yet Miss Bates is never held up to ridicule. This is why Emma's mockery at Box Hill is so jarring.

Miss Bates is a lady full of good-will and kindness and this makes Emma's cruelty shocking. The economic situation of the ladies is full of pathos and thus, Miss Bates is deserving of respect.

John and Isabella Knightley

John and Isabella are a very ordinary but happy married couple. Isabella is 'a pretty, elegant little woman, of gentle, quiet manners and a disposition remarkably amiable and affectionate'. (Chapter 11) She is devoted to her husband and is a good but overprotective mother of five children. She is not clever like Emma. She is contented in her domestic situation and overlooks her husband's occasional sharpness.

John is 'a tall, gentleman-like, and very clever man'. (Chapter 11) He is more reserved by nature than his brother, George. He is sometimes sharp in his replies to his wife or to Mr Woodhouse and Emma is privately critical of this. However, the interchange between Mr Woodhouse and John and Isabella in Chapter 12 cannot fail to make the reader sympathise with John Knightley's irritations. He does not particularly enjoy social occasions and is out of sorts when they go to Randalls for dinner on Christmas Eve. He is a good father and clearly enjoys being with his children.

John observes Mr Elton's behaviour when the curate is with Emma and feels her manners towards him are too encouraging. Emma typically discounts his observations in favour of her own, and is shortly proved wrong.

Robert Martin

Robert Martin, the young tenant farmer who loves and eventually marries Harriet Smith, is a respectable young man, who according to Mr Knightley, 'always speaks to the purpose' and is 'open, straight forward, and very well judging'. (Chapter 8) He reads, he writes well, and in every way, is a most respectable, commendable young man. His farm, Abbey Mill Farm, is obviously prosperous and it is clear that he is an upwardly mobile young man and will be able to provide a comfortable life for a wife.

Emma is blind to all of his positive qualities, describing him cruelly as 'clownish' and 'illiterate and coarse'. (Chapter 4) He remains in love with Harriet, despite her initial refusal of his proposal. Seeing her in London with Isabella and John Knightley gives him the opportunity to speak to her again and this time, she accepts him.

When the truth of Harriet's parentage emerges; she is the daughter of a tradesman, not a gentleman, it is clear that she has made a very favourable match. Harriet will be 'respectable and happy' and her home with Robert Martin will promise 'security, stability, and improvement'. (Chapter 55)

Characters as Foils

It can be a useful exercise to consider the characters in pairs, as this raises interesting questions about them individually. Mrs Elton is a foil for Emma. Both seek to occupy the top of the social ladder in Highbury and both are snobbish. Emma is critical of Mrs Elton's interference in Jane Fairfax's affairs, yet she does just this with Harriet. Emma's faults are reflected in Mrs Elton.

Jane Fairfax can also be seen as foil for Emma. She is far more accomplished than Emma and demonstrates the result of sustained effort in the acquisition of skills. Emma is jealous of Jane, as her accomplishments reveal Emma's inability to persist with tasks whether reading, music or painting. Her character can be seen as steadier than Emma's. Emma is rich while Jane is poor. Thus Emma has greater freedom and independence while Jane is constrained both by her poverty and by her secret engagement.

Frank Churchill is a foil for Mr Knightley. Frank is charming and has a gift with repartee, while Mr Knightley is plainly spoken and makes no effort to charm. Frank is devious, while Mr Knightley is honest. Emma comes to realise 'Mr Knightley's high superiority of character' when she compares them at the end of the novel. (Chapter 54)

Reflect on these questions:

1. Which aspects of Emma's character incline the reader to empathy?
2. Emma muses that 'it was really too much to hope even of Harriet, that she could be in love with more than three men in one year'. What does this reveal of Harriet and of Emma?
3. Who are the strong or influential women in *Emma* and how do they reveal and exert their power?
4. Does George Knightley set the moral standard in *Emma*?
5. Are Mr Knightley's perceptions of Frank skewed by personal bias and thus unreliable? Or does he intuit Frank's shallow and manipulative character right from the beginning?
6. How does Frank Churchill fall short of being a true gentleman?
7. Why is Frank Churchill's duplicity excused and forgiven by everyone? Has he changed by the end of the novel?
8. Compare Mr Elton and Mr Knightley. How does this illuminate their virtues and faults?
9. Both Emma and Frank Churchill attempt to manipulate people and situations. How does Austen position the reader to be sympathetic to Emma yet critical of Frank?
10. Are the various couples — Emma and Mr Knightley, Jane Fairfax and Frank Churchill, Harriet and Robert Martin — well matched or ill matched?

Themes

Self-knowledge

In Chapter 1, the narrator tells us that 'the real evils of Emma's situation were the power of having rather too much of her own way, a disposition to think too well of herself'. Emma at this point in the novel can be described as narcissistic, snobbish, confident in her view of the world, but unable to judge character or understand her own heart. Gradually, through a series of blunders and near disasters, Emma acquires both self-knowledge and a greater ability to see other people more clearly.

After manipulating Harriet into rejecting Robert Martin, Emma observes the supposed courtship between her protégé and Mr Elton with satisfaction, and manages to rationalise away any hint that the young man's affections are not totally engaged. Thus, she is blind to the real object of Mr Elton's interest and his proposal is both unexpected and unwelcome.

Emma's realisation that her schemes have hurt Harriet brings contrition. She agonises over her 'mis-judgement' and 'blunders'. 'She had taken up an idea, she supposed, and made everything to bend to it.' She resolves at this point 'to do such things no more.' (Chapter 16) But although her feelings are acute at this point, her resolve does not last.

Emma does not know her own heart. She convinces herself that she is in love with Frank Churchill. She mistakes missing the enjoyment of Frank's company for missing Frank himself. Frank has livened up the usually staid routines of Emma's world and she feels when he leaves, that everything is 'dull and insipid about the house'. (Chapter 27) On this slim evidence, Emma believes herself in love. Tellingly, she sees no long-term continuation of this love. By the time Frank returns, Emma's feelings have 'subsided into a mere nothing', but she is convinced that he is in love with her. (Chapter 37) In Emma's defence, it can be pointed out that both the Westons and Mr Knightley also believe that Frank is showing her all the attentions of a lover. All are deceived.

Emma at this point has refrained from active matchmaking on Harriet's behalf, but still uses Harriet's faith in her greater wisdom to give her permission to 'raise her thoughts' to a lover of higher social rank. She advises her that 'more wonderful things have taken place, there have been matches of greater disparity'. (Chapter 40) Emma is mistaken as to the object of Harriet's thoughts.

The incident at Box Hill is the turning point in Emma's growth in self-awareness. The realisation that she has been thoughtlessly 'so brutal, so cruel' to Miss Bates shows ugly aspects of Emma's character to herself. She looks back on her relationship with Miss Bates and her self-examination shows her that she has often been 'scornful, ungracious'. (Chapter 44) She resolves to make amends and we feel that this time, her contrition will be more lasting.

The revelation of Frank Churchill and Jane Fairfax's secret engagement further discomforts Emma. Her certainty that Frank was in love with her has proved unfounded and his attentions were 'a system of hypocrisy and deceit'. (Chapter 46) This shock is followed by a greater one. The object of Harriet's love is not Frank Churchill, but Mr Knightley. This knowledge has a two-fold result. Emma finally understands that she loves Mr Knightley, and she sees her own past conduct in all its arrogance and insensitivity.

The reader knows that all ends well and happily for Emma, but only after she has learned some mortifying lessons. She has seen the consequences of her self-confessed 'arrogance' and 'vanity'. (Chapter 47) She has admitted her faults to herself and resolved on improved conduct. The reader feels that this time the remorse will have lasting effects.

Marriage and Gender

Emma begins with a marriage and ends with three. In between, there is preoccupation with marriage. There are expectations of marriages, thwarted marriages and actual marriages. Yet it is not marriage in itself which is the focus in *Emma*. Austen is not interested in 'happy ever after' scenarios. The various entanglements, disentanglements and eventual matches are the means by which character is revealed, perceptions are changed, lessons are learned and self-knowledge is gained.

Marriage was the accepted social norm among Georgian/Regency England's gentry. Men married to preserve or improve their social and financial status. Women married to achieve a position of security. Young women, of little means, needed to marry or to spend their lives dependent on the charity of male relatives or as a governess. All of these factors underlie the plot development in *Emma.*

Mr Elton's pursuit of Emma is an attempt to improve his social and financial status. After the disastrous proposal, Emma reflects that 'he wanted to marry well', 'he wanted to aggrandize and enrich himself' and if he could not secure 'Miss Woodhouse of Hartfield, the heiress of thirty thousand pounds', 'he would try for Miss Somebody else with twenty, or with ten'. (Chapter 16) He quickly finds Miss Augusta Hawkins, the daughter of a merchant. She has a fortune of ten thousand pounds, so Mr Elton is exceedingly pleased with the match. His bride is a foolish woman, socially inept and small-minded. Mr Knightley comments after the ball that Harriet would have made a better partner for him and that Emma 'would have chosen for him better than he has chosen for himself'. (Chapter 38) However, Mr Elton's priority in choosing his spouse was not the possession of admirable qualities, but the possession of money. In fact, the Eltons are well suited in their pettiness. *Emma* shows that finding a spouse can be quite a cynical undertaking.

In contrast to Mr Elton's elevation, the possible marriage between Mr Knightley and Harriet would be 'a debasement', which would cause 'sneers' and 'merriment' among their acquaintances and 'mortification' for his family. The discrepancy between the landowner and 'the natural daughter of somebody' would be a scandal. Emma, aware by this point that she loves Mr Knightley, is prepared to give up any hope of marrying him if only this disastrous union is averted. Her desires are unselfish and show how far she has progressed from the self-centred young woman at the beginning of the novel.

Modern readers may be uncomfortable with Emma's desire to 'grow more worthy of him, whose intentions and judgement had ever been so superior to her own'. (Chapter 54) It does not seem to speak of equality, but almost as though Emma is marrying a father figure. However, readers of Austen's day would not have objected to the idea of a husband, superior in education and life experience. Women, restricted to a smaller world and limited education, had little chance to broaden their horizons.

The majority of women in the gentry needed to marry to secure themselves financially. However, Emma has no need to marry. She is sufficiently wealthy to have independence and security. She is already mistress of her father's home. Marriage could take away this independence. Only love will change her mind. For her, marriage will be a choice, not something thrust on her by economic necessity. Emma's defence of single womanhood has interested feminist critics. The limitations placed on women by marriage and motherhood seem less for a woman of means.

By contrast, Miss Bates lives with the reality of being unmarried and poor. Dwindling finances have reduced her circumstances and she depends on the charity of such as the Woodhouses and Mr Knightley for hospitality and gifts of food which she and her mother could not otherwise afford. Harriet is horrified when Emma says she will never marry as she sees Miss Bates' situation as the future for all old maids. In fact, she and Jane Fairfax face an uncertain future if they do not marry. Jane is contemplating being a governess if the marriage to Frank does not eventuate. She has no fortune to attract another good match. It is clear how much Jane loathes the idea of being a governess as she compares the situation with the slave trade. Yet, she has no other option if she does not marry. Harriet Smith is in danger of marrying disastrously if she does not marry Robert Martin. Poverty is a real prospect for these two women.

What messages about marriage might be discovered in the novel? The main one could be that affection is necessary, along with similar values. This does not negate the economic and social realities of marriage. Emma and Mr Knightley are equals intellectually and they talk freely. They are also appropriately matched in economic and social status. There is no sense that Emma is submitting in any way to Mr Knightley. Other good marriages are between Mr and Mrs Weston and between Harriet Smith and Robert Martin. Robert Martin has continued to be in love with Harriet and she rediscovers her feelings for him once she is no longer in Emma's orbit. Although 'her connections may be worse than his', there is no great gap in their situations.

The novel makes clear that some women have to settle for second best. Jane Fairfax is in love with Frank, but he has an inferior character to hers. He has already persuaded her to act contrary to her conscience. Jane is an intelligent woman and so is possibly aware of his shortcomings. However, the alternative is dire. Mr Knightley hopes that Jane will improve Frank and that he is lucky to have been accepted by her. The reader is left to ponder what their future may be like.

Some feminist critics have seen the actual or virtual motherless state of some of Austen's heroines, including Emma, Harriet and Jane Fairfax, as leading them to place their trust in men for security. However, the issue does not seem so simple. The patriarchal system left women few options but to marry, and hopefully, marry well.

Critics have argued over whether Austen was conservative, accepting the status quo, or radical, wishing to subvert it. Some have seen Emma as giving up her power and submitting to the patriarchal system. (In fact, Mr Knightley gives up some of his power by the compromise of living at Hartfield.) Others have seen the marriage of Emma and Mr Knightley as a pairing of equals. The reader must decide for themselves on these questions.

Social Class

An understanding of the social structures of Emma's world is essential to understanding the characters, events and issues of the novel. Social position is based on rank in society as well as wealth. The first chapter reveals the way in which Highbury and its environs has levels of social strata clearly understood by everyone. The Woodhouses and Mr Knightley are at the top of the social ladder and Emma revels in her position. Those in their enviable position enjoy wealth, an easy life cared for by numbers of servants and freedom of action, but they also have obligations. The Woodhouses not only extend hospitality to those below them socially (the Bates, Mrs Goddard), but are generous with gifts of food (joints of meat). As well, Emma is expected to visit some of the poor of the village and to be similarly generous with donations of food, although the food is of a more basic type (bone broth) as befits their lowly status. We also observe Mr Knightley fulfilling his obligations to his tenants, the duty of an honourable and fair landowner.

Emma abuses her prominent social standing by her insulting comment to Miss Bates. Emma has a duty to behave respectfully and compassionately towards someone who is well-bred, but has fallen socially due to dwindling finances.

When Mrs Elton arrives in Highbury, she competes with Emma for the superior place in Highbury society. She ostentatiously wears pearls on two occasions. Pearls have long associations with the royalty and the aristocracy, and through wearing them she attempts to signal her perception of her elevated status. Mrs Elton believes that money alone will secure her the prestige she desires. She constantly refers to her sister and brother-in-law, the Sucklings, who have an estate, to suggest a higher status for herself than she actually enjoys as the daughter of someone in trade.

Mrs Elton is brash and insensitive, and unknowingly violates the social code by assuming an unwarranted familiarity with people. She calls Mr Knightley 'Knightley' and refers to Mr Woodhouse as 'this dear old beau of mine'. Fortunately for Mrs Elton, most of the Highbury community, with the exception of Emma and Mr Knightley, regard her quite benignly.

In Austen's day, the Industrial Revolution and the wealth created by trade was beginning to slightly moderate the rigidity of social structures. We learn that Mr Weston has improved his position by success in trade which has enabled the purchase of a modest property. In turn, Miss Taylor's marriage to him has elevated her socially from the position of a governess to that of the wife of a small landowner. The Coles have also improved their social standing by continued success in trade, enabling them to enjoy a higher standard of living. Emma is initially unwilling to accept a dinner invitation from the Coles because in her snobbish way, she believes that they should not presume to invite superior families to dine with them and need to be taught a 'lesson'! She capitulates as everyone else in Highbury is happy to dine with them, although she refers to her acceptance as 'condescension' and reflects on how happy her presence at their dinner table must have made them.

Mrs Elton's background is from trade, but it obvious to the reader that whereas Mr Weston and the Coles are acceptable, Mrs Elton is not. Mrs Elton's vulgarity and presumption are the problem, not her background. These characteristics militate against the acceptance more easily achieved by the Westons and the Coles.

While in Austen's day social class was becoming more fluid, Emma's efforts on Harriet's behalf show the unfortunate consequences of trying to elevate someone too far beyond their class level. Emma's foolish plans are based on the idea that Harriet must be the daughter of a gentleman. She places Harriet in a class to which she does not belong and proceeds on that mistaken premise. Similarly, Mr Elton makes erroneous assumptions about the class from which he may seek a bride. Emma is too far above him. It is ironic that he is horrified at Emma's attempt to match him with Harriet, while at the same time Emma is horrified at his aspirations. Both are appalled at the discrepancies of rank.

Emma realises the folly of raising Harriet's expectations too far beyond her actual social class, when she contemplates a marriage between Harriet and Mr Knightley. The match would be wonderful for Harriet, but disastrous socially for Mr Knightley.

Jane Fairfax is a penniless member of the minor gentry and her lack of any wealth ensures that Mrs Churchill will not countenance a match with Frank Churchill. Thus, the engagement must be secret. The marriage when it eventually occurs will be one of great disparity.

Perceptions and Misperceptions

Our perceptions of the world are coloured by our experiences, beliefs, attitudes, fears and desires. Thus perceptions may be unreliable. In *Emma*, there are a number of examples of reliance on flawed perceptions. In each case, the misperception leads to unpleasant and upsetting consequences.

Emma perceives Elton as interested in Harriet, not in her. Likewise, she believes Frank Churchill is in love with her. She thinks Harriet is aspiring to Frank Churchill when it is actually Mr Knightley who is the object of her affections. Finally, she perceives Mr Knightley as being in love with Harriet, not with her.

Emma's perception of herself is as a skilful matchmaker. She attempts to foster what she sees a growing attachment between Mr Elton and Harriet by friendly overtures and frequent invitations to Hartfield. These are misconstrued by him as encouragement and a good basis on which to propose to her. Emma and Mr Elton suffer under flawed perceptions, influenced by their desires.

Early in the novel, Emma's view of Mr Elton is that he is a pleasant young man, though perhaps a little implausible in his efforts to be charming. The incident at the Highbury ball reveals his true character to her. 'There is a littleness about him which you discovered, and which I did not', she tells Mr Knightley. (Chapter 38) Her original perception of Mr Elton was coloured by her wishes to cast him in the role of Harriet's future husband. Observation of his ungallant action corrects this mistaken opinion of him.

Harriet raises her eyes to Mr Knightley after being inadvertently encouraged by Emma. She perceives his increased friendliness towards her as proof of his growing affection. In turn, Emma's awareness of this greater attention seems to support the contention that Harriet is correct. In this case, the flawed perceptions are influenced by desire on Harriet's part and fear on Emma's.

Emma accepts Frank Churchill's attentions as genuine. Fortunately, after an initial mild flurry of feeling towards him, she does not allow her emotions to be engaged. However, the Westons and Mr Knightley believe that she is attracted to Frank and are concerned on her behalf when the truth is revealed. Their perceptions of the situation are coloured respectively by desire and fear. The Westons desire a match between Frank and Emma and perceive the young people's interactions as proof of growing attachment. Mr Knightley is jealous of Frank and fears that Emma is becoming close to him.

Mrs Elton's perception of her rightful place in Highbury society is flawed. She expects to set the standard for appropriate social behaviour. She is completely unaware of when she oversteps boundaries, her delusions aided by the generally benign perception of her by many in Highbury.

Trust and Deceit

Frank Churchill immediately comes to mind when the issue of 'trust and deceit' is considered in *Emma*. Welcomed and accepted into the community of Highbury, he betrays this trust in him. The outwardly open and pleasing manner conceals months of double-dealing. Only Mr Knightley is not charmed by Frank. When his devious behaviour is revealed, he comments, 'I would still have distrusted him.' (Chapter 51)

Jane Fairfax is a party to Frank's deceit. Against her sense of what is right, she enters into the secret engagement, trusting Frank's judgement that this is their only course of action. Because of this, she must play the part of a mere acquaintance of Frank, deceiving her grandmother, aunt, and all of her acquaintance in Highbury.

In *Emma*, misplaced trust leads to unwanted consequences. Harriet places great trust in Emma's judgement. As Mr Knightley comments, 'She knows nothing herself and looks upon Emma as knowing every thing.' (Chapter 5)

She is a little dazzled by the attention from Miss Woodhouse who is 'so great a personage in Highbury' (Chapter 3) and trusting her, rejects Robert Martin, to whom she is quite clearly attracted, and allows herself to be directed towards Mr Elton. Emma encourages her focus on him and when she is rejected by Mr Elton, Harriet suffers. Later in the novel, she believes Emma's assurance that matches of great disparity are possible and raises her eyes to Mr Knightley. Fortunately, when she is removed to London, away from Emma's influence, she is able to trust her own judgement and to accept Robert Martin's proposal.

Emma begins the novel by implicitly trusting in the truth of her own observations and the wisdom of her decisions. With no real evidence, she believes that Harriet is the daughter of a gentleman. Disregarding Mr Knightley's words of warning about Mr Elton, she continues with her schemes for Harriet. She interprets all the interactions of Harriet and Mr Elton as proof of his interest. She is disconcerted when John Knightley suggests that Mr Elton is interested in her, not in Harriet and reassures herself, ironically, 'in the consideration of the blunders which often arise from a partial knowledge of the circumstances, of the mistakes which people of high pretensions to judgement are ever falling into'. (Chapter 13) At this point, Emma trusts her own observations over other people's views of the same situation.

Similarly, Emma trusts her observations of Frank Churchill's behaviour as evidence that he is in love with her. Frank, for his part, excuses the way he has acted towards Emma by claiming that he believed she was 'indifferent' to him and that they understood each other. (Chapter 50) In other words, he claims that a measure of trust existed between them. Frank's defence of his own behaviour in this way is a very convenient way of absolving himself from accusations of deceitful behaviour.

Emma trusts Mr Knightley's judgement, except when it runs counter to her own. As she grows in self-knowledge, she trusts her own judgement less and is more open to criticism. The incident at Box Hill is a catalyst for this change. She accepts Mr Knightley's upbraiding and realises the truth of what he says.

Reflect on these questions:

1. What does *Emma* reveal about the relationship between marriage and money?
2. Is marriage portrayed in a positive or negative light in *Emma*?
3. What examples of gender expectations can you find? Can you surmise Jane Austen's attitude to the limitations of gender from them?
4. Some critics have seen Jane Austen as conservative in her approach to the social order of her day. Others have seen her as wishing to subvert it. What is your view?
5. Is there any evidence in *Emma* that Jane Austen is concerned with the social divisions of her society?
6. What lessons does *Emma* teach us about relying on appearances?
7. What other themes can you discover in *Emma*?

Setting

Jane Austen's novels, including *Emma*, are set in rural England in the late Georgian era. Highbury is the fictional village in which or close to which most of the characters live. Various other localities – London, Bath, Richmond, Southend, Weymouth, Maple Grove and Enscomb (Yorkshire) are mentioned, but no plot events occur in these places.

Jane Austen has few descriptions of setting for their own sake in her novels. Usually they relate to or illuminate the characters in some way.

Highbury is supposedly set in Surrey, about sixteen miles from central London, nine miles from Richmond and seven miles from Box Hill. Emma has never been very far from Highbury as her father dislikes travelling. Because of this insularity, Emma has limited life experience.

Highbury is a close-knit community, in which people of a similar class know and visit each other, and gossip disseminates quickly. The various visits which people make constantly to each other reveal the level of friendship or social obligation between them. For example, Mr Knightley is a frequent visitor to Hartfield. He drops in without an invitation, which shows that he and the Woodhouses are on a similar social level. (He also calls often because he likes to see Emma!) Again, Emma calls on Miss Bates, but the Bates ladies only come to Hartfield when invited. Emma finds visits to the Bates irksome, but after Box Hill, she resolves to be more attentive and compassionate to them. Frank Churchill is a master at contriving visits with plausible excuses to see Jane.

There is an openness in this community of Highbury, and the secretiveness brought in by Frank Churchill and Jane Fairfax is at odds with it.

Hartfield is only separated from Highbury by a 'separate lawn and shrubberies' so Emma has easy access to the village on her walks. The Woodhouse family is 'first in consequence' in Highbury and Emma has no female friends on an equal basis in the village.

Ford's is the village shop where people meet and chat. We know the shop sells fabric of various kinds, other materials needed for sewing, and gloves as Frank Churchill buys some there. It sells many other items which are not mentioned. When Emma stands at the door of Ford's, she looks down the main street of Highbury and observes the butcher, the baker and Cox's law office. Mr Perry is seen walking quickly, so we can infer that he has rooms close by, too.

Randalls is the small estate adjoining Highbury. The Westons live here and it is sufficiently close to allow frequent visits between the Woodhouses and the Westons. It is not as large as Hartfield and Mrs Weston is anxious when Mr Weston raises the possibility of everyone staying on Christmas Eve because of the snow. It has 'but two spare rooms'. (Chapter 15)

Donwell Abbey is the home of Mr George Knightley. It is about a mile from Highbury. It is a larger estate than Hartfield. Mr Knightley is the local magistrate or squire and his house is in keeping with his status in the community. When Emma visits, she is pleased with 'the respectable size and style of the building' and its ample gardens stretching down to meadows washed by a stream'. (Chapter 42) This is one of the few places in the novel when we are provided with a number of clear visual images. Emma feels affection for the place because of her unacknowledged affection for the owner.

Brunswick Square is the London home of John and Isabella Knightley. It is a respectable, but not fashionable area. Isabella and John's house possibly had access to the gardens that were close by, giving substance to Isabella's claim that it is 'remarkably airy' in that area. (Chapter 12)

Bath is a city in south-west England. It is a stylish and popular vacation spot, and people often avail themselves of the spa there for health reasons.

Richmond is on the outskirts of London and an easy ride to Highbury for Frank.

Southend is a south-east coastal town, popular at the time for the 'sea-bathing' thought to be so beneficial for health. It is forty miles from London. Discussion of the merits of South End cause discord between Mr Woodhouse and his son-in-law.

Abbey Mill Farm is the home of the Martins. Harriet is impressed by the Martins having 'two very good parlours', so the house is obviously quite comfortable. When Emma visits Donwell Abbey, she observes Abbey Mill Farm and is favourably impressed with its 'appendages of prosperity and beauty, its rich pastures, spreading flocks, orchard in blossom, and light column of smoke ascending'. (Chapter 42) As with the earlier description of Donwell Abbey, these positive images lay the groundwork for Emma's happy acceptance of Harriet and Robert's match later in the novel.

Weymouth is a popular seaside vacation spot, south of London. It was overtaking Bath as the stylish place to go. It is the place where Frank and Jane met.

Enscomb is the Yorkshire home of the Churchills. It is 190 miles from London, a very long journey in those days. Frank Churchill initially needs to stay at Randalls for longer periods because of the length of the journey between the two. The Churchills move to Richmond because of Mrs Churchill's failing health and Frank is more easily able to visit Highbury.

Enscomb is associated with the dominating presence of Mrs Churchill for most of the novel. After her death and the proposal, Enscomb has more pleasant associations.

Maple Grove is the home of Mrs Elton's sister and brother-in-law, the Sucklings. It is more than a hundred miles from London. Mrs Elton constantly refers to it as evidence of a close connection with people with an estate.

The Crown Inn is where the ball is held. In the past when more balls were held at Highbury, a ball-room was added. This gives Frank the idea of having a ball. Many meetings are held at the Crown and the local whist club meets there.

The poorer classes do not figure largely in the novel. Emma visits a poor family on Vicarage Road as part of her duties as a gentlewoman. The reader has no idea of what their housing might have been like. The gypsies appear briefly as a threat to be overcome by the dashing Frank, but again, there is no description of their housing.

Narrative Techniques

Examination of the plot of *Emma* reveals three sections. The first section covers the events involving Emma, Harriet, Robert Martin and Mr Elton. The second section concerns Emma, Frank Churchill and Jane Fairfax, and the interactions both open and hidden between them. The last section reveals the secret engagement, and matches Emma and Knightley, and Harriet Smith and Robert Martin. Throughout this, Emma is present in almost every chapter, and it is her thoughts, feelings, actions and reactions which provide unity.

In the first section, Emma is full of confidence in the rightness of her perceptions of the world around her. This confidence is shaken by the knowledge that she has been mistaken in her observations of Mr Elton. She resolves to cease her manipulations on Harriet's part. The second section examines the impact of the arrival of both Jane Fairfax and Frank Churchill in Highbury. Frank pays great attention to Emma as a cover for his actual relationship with Jane. Emma, again confident in her perceptions, believes he is in love with her. A secondary thread in this section is the arrival back in Highbury of Mr Elton and his appalling bride. The third section reveals yet more of Emma's misperceptions and the Box Hill incident which is the true pivotal point in her self-growth. The novel moves to its conclusion with the revelation of the secret engagement and two proposals.

Within the novel, six parties are devices which move the plot along. Each party is an opportunity for some significant event or development. The first party is the Christmas Eve dinner at Randalls. This is the scene for Mr Elton's unexpected and unwelcome proposal. At the Coles' party, the mystery of the gift of the piano is raised. Emma hosts a dinner party for Mrs Elton, where she begins to put pressure on Jane to look around for a governess's position. The fourth party is the dance at the Crown Inn. It is here that Mr Elton slights Harriet and Mr Knightley rescues her from embarrassment, inadvertently causing her to become infatuated with him. The Donwell Abbey strawberry picking party sees Emma looking at both Donwell Abbey and at Abbey Mill Farm with approval, foreshadowing both her future and that of Harriet. As well, the inexplicable behaviour of both Jane Fairfax and Frank Churchill creates a mystery for the reader. Finally, the disaster of Box Hill sees Emma's unconscionable insult to Miss Bates.

Jane Austen has a precise and formal writing style, rich in irony. She is generally credited as the first novelist to use free indirect discourse to a great extent. The narrative voice assumes the speech of the character. The character's thoughts, feelings and words are filtered through the third person narrator.

With this device, there is potential for ambiguity in separating the voices of characters from the narrative voice. Often the similarity between the spirited voice of the narrator and Emma's voice may lead to misreading. There is still debate among critics over whose voice we are hearing in particular sections of the novel. The reader must pay careful attention to whose voice they are hearing and make a decision based on their own interpretation of the characters.

As Emma's self-awareness grows, she is able to incorporate others' voices into her own. An example of this is in Chapter 47 where she reflects on her misguidance of Harriet:

> 'Poor Harriet! to be a second time the dupe of her misconceptions and flattery. Mr Knightley had spoken prophetically, when he once said, "Emma, you have been no friend to Harriet Smith."— She was afraid she had done her nothing but disservice.'

The ability to look back and remember ruefully the comment, which at the time she had archly dismissed and to realise the truth of it, is evidence of how fully her conscience has awakened. In her earlier monologues, the reader has heard only Emma's voice. The incorporation of Mr Knightley's comment shows that Emma has become less overweeningly confident and self-centred, and more aware of the validity of other people's opinions.

The omniscient narrator guides the reader's opinions. The critic, Mary Lascelles, has pointed out that Austen is self-effacing as a narrator and thus is completely unobtrusive. Yet, Austen manipulates our point of view so that we never lose sympathy with Emma. Despite our annoyance at times with her snobbishness and blindness, the sharing of her perceptions, emotions and reflections keeps the reader interested in and concerned for her.

Similarly, the narrator positions the reader to approve or disapprove of particular characters. These do not always accord with the sentiments expressed by the community of Highbury. We are meant to be appalled by

Mrs Elton's pretensions, but the community perception is in alignment with Mr Woodhouse that she is 'a very pretty sort of young woman'. (Chapter 32)

Characters are created not by direct descriptions, but through their words, actions, thoughts, relationships and through other characters' viewpoints. Austen conveys much of the personality of each character through their manner of speaking and their choice of words. Mr Woodhouse becomes associated in the reader's mind with the word 'poor' and with concerns about draughts and chills.

Harriet's indecision and constant reliance on Emma's guidance is encapsulated in her ramblings in Ford's:

> "…Then if you please, you shall send it all to Mrs. Goddard's—I do not know—No, I think, Miss Woodhouse, I may as well have it sent to Hartfield, and take it home with me at night. What do you advise?" (Chapter 27)

Mrs Elton's speech is full of self-promotion and repeated allusions to her more wealthy relatives. There is irony in the frequent instances of her contradicting herself. She gives a little homily on her liking for simplicity—'I have the greatest dislike to the idea of being over-trimmed—quite a horror of finery'—and then proposes over-trimming what sounds to be a simple dress. (Chapter 35)

Mr Elton's proposal to Emma is an excessive parody of a proposal. He declares he is 'hoping—fearing—adoring—ready to die if she refused him; but flattering himself that his ardent attachment and unequalled love and unexampled passion could not fail of having some effect'. (Chapter 15) The sentiments are ridiculous and it is obvious to Emma and the reader that he means none of it.

The garrulous, but well-meaning Miss Bates is presented by long monologues, composed of truncated sentences and moving from one subject to another and back again. The reader can hear her breathless excitement at the prospect of Jane's imminent visit and at the same time appreciate how wearing this good lady's company might be. Emma parodies Miss Bates' conversation about a possible match between Mr Knightley and Jane Fairfax and has the nuances exactly right, providing rather cruel humour at her expense. (Chapter 26)

Language has changed in many ways since Austen's time. The meaning of some words, e.g. 'pretty' and 'handsome'. Mr Woodhouse calls Mr Elton 'a very pretty young man' and simply means that he is a pleasant in appearance. (Chapter 1) Emma is described as 'handsome'. This adjective is not now usually applied to a woman. Again, Frank Churchill is reported as having written a 'handsome' letter. This suggests that the letter has contained very agreeable sentiments. Syntax has also changed since Jane Austen's day and this can make the thoughts difficult to follow.

There are various types of irony in *Emma*. *Situational irony*, the disconnection between what one thinks and what is actually the reality, is evident throughout the novel. For example:

- Emma's perception of herself as a matchmaker and the reality that she is just meddling where she should not.
- Emma's belief that Mr Elton is pursuing Harriet when Emma, herself, is the object of his attentions.
- Emma's encouragement of Mr Elton on Harriet's behalf which he interprets as encouragement to him.
- Emma's certainty that Frank Churchill is in love with her, when he is in love with Jane Fairfax.
- Mr Knightley's fear that Emma is in love with Frank Churchill when she is in love with him.
- Emma's fear that Mr Knightley is in love with Harriet when he is in love with her.

The picture of Harriet painted by Emma is an example of situational irony. Mr Knightley criticises it as Harriet has been depicted as too tall in it. Emma's unrealistic portrait of Harriet reflects her unrealistic view of her friend's prospects in the marriage market. There is a disconnection between what Emma thinks and what the reality is. The portrait is a metaphor for this.

Dramatic irony, when the reader has knowledge that the characters do not, is also at work in *Emma*. Dramatic irony often blends with situational irony. At the commencement of *Emma*, the reader is positioned to see Emma as indulged and having 'too much of her own way'. Her plans for Harriet are selfish and the reader fears, misguided. It is clear that she is no skilful matchmaker. It is equally clear that Robert Martin is a perfectly acceptable young man and a good match for Harriet. The working out of the comedy of errors which follows is always against the background of the reader's early knowledge.

The reader will be amused at Emma's outrage over Mrs Elton's patronage of Jane Fairfax, as it is apparent that this mirrors Emma's efforts for her protégé, Harriet. The irony resides in her lack of awareness that she is equally meddlesome.

The astute reader will suspect Mr Knightley's interest in Emma from the way he becomes irritated at any favourable mention of Frank Churchill by Emma. Emma is often bemused by his reactions, but the reader is not.

It is ironic that Emma, who is so concerned with others' love affairs, cannot tell whether or not she is in love. She concludes that she is in love with Frank on specious evidence. The reader can very clearly see that she is not in the least in love. By contrast, she cannot tell that she loves Mr Knightley until Harriet's declaration, yet the astute reader will see the signs long before that.

Verbal irony takes different forms. It is used for both comic and satiric purposes. When Emma, Mr Knightley and Mr Woodhouse have tea after the proposal, Mr Woodhouse is anxious for his friend's health. The narrator comments that 'Could he have seen the heart, he would have cared very little for the lungs'. (Chapter 50). The humour here is the contrast between Mr Woodhouse's preoccupations and Mr Knightley's. As well, it relies on the reader's knowledge of Mr Woodhouse's hypochondria.

Austen uses antithesis for comic effect. An example is 'Emma denied none of it aloud, and agreed to none of it in private.' (Chapter 42) Emma is extremely provoked by Mr Weston, and this sentence reveals the gap between her public demeanour and her private emotion.

Humour is created in other ways besides irony in Emma. Sometimes, it is provided by the foibles of characters: Mr Woodhouse's determination to guard the health of his visitors by preventing them from eating well and his frequent wish for everyone to partake of gruel, or Mrs Elton's wish to play the Arcadian shepherdess at the strawberry picking party. Sometimes, humour is provided by the voice of the narrator as in this description of Mr Knightley's feelings at the end of Chapter 49. His opinion of Frank Churchill is juxtaposed with Emma's responses to him, Mr Knightley.

> 'He had found her agitated and low.—Frank Churchill was a villain.—He heard her declare that she had never loved him.—Frank Churchill's character was not desperate.—She was his own Emma, by hand and word, when they returned into the house; and if he could have thought of Frank Churchill then, he might have deemed him a very good sort of fellow.'

A number of symbols are employed in *Emma*. The riddle or charade which Mr Elton gives Emma and Harriet, and intended for Emma, not Harriet can be seen as a symbol of Emma's blindness and refusal to see anything beyond her own desires. The word game played by Emma, Frank and Jane in Chapter 41, is a symbol of the game being played by the three. Jane and Frank are aware that they are involved in subterfuge, but Emma, not at all. Letters are a symbol of Frank's ability to keep both his parents and Emma happy by remaining at a distance and communicating by letter, something he excels at. They are the secret way Frank and Jane communicate and her returning his letters to him signals the finality of her decision to break off the engagement.

Reflect on these questions:

1. Some critics have seen Austen as ridiculing her characters. Do you find any evidence for this?
2. Examine the language of Frank Churchill and Mr Knightley. What is revealed about each of them by their speech and choice of words?
3. Contrast the language of Mr Elton's proposal with the language of Mr Knightley's. What does the language reveal of both of them?
4. How does the dialogue of particular characters, e.g. Mr Woodhouse, Mrs Elton, Miss Bates, sway how we feel about them?

Textual Integrity

Textual integrity is the overall unity of a text achieved when form and language work in harmony to produce a cohesive whole which has meaning and value.

To come to your own decision about the textual integrity of *Emma*, ask yourself a number of questions. If you find that you answer any question in the negative, consider how much this affects the novels' textual integrity. Is Emma, the protagonist, a realistic character? Does she develop through the course of the novel and in so doing, retain the reader's interest and empathy? Are there any characters who seem implausible or who are extraneous to the action of the plot?

Are there any events in the plot which you find unnecessary or unbelievable? For example, is it credible that Mrs Churchill dies at a very convenient time for Frank Churchill? Is the structure of the plot an essential element in creating a unified whole?

How do the language and narrative techniques of *Emma*, e.g. symbols or motifs reinforce the internal cohesion of the text? Does the ironic point of view strengthen or detract from this cohesion?

All of Jane Austen's novels are part of the canon of English literature and *Emma* continues to be read, discussed and valued more than two hundred years after it was first published. Valued texts deal with aspects of the human condition which do not change over time: love, loss, growth, change, fear, and so on. What universal themes and concerns can be discovered in *Emma* which have led to its inclusion in the canon? Are these themes adequately revealed and supported by character development and language techniques in *Emma?*

After considering these questions, decide whether you can make a case for, or against textual integrity. Do all the elements work together to create a homogenous entity or are there aspects which you feel jar or do not fit? What is your view?

Film and Television Versions of *Emma*

There have been numerous film and television adaptations of *Emma*. In film versions, the ironic narrator is replaced by added dialogue and by emphasis on facial expression and body language. This is not totally satisfactory as a pronouncement by the narrator can sound jarring or unconvincing when put into the mouth of a character.

As well, the modern bias of the screenwriter, director and actors can make the audience's experience of a film different to the reader's experience of the novel. In particular, modern versions often cater to the audience's ideas of a classless society and introduce scenes and lines which are at variance with the novel and the social reality of the day.

The restricted length of a film and the need to hurry along or combine events inevitably means that subtle aspects of the novel's plot may be lost.

The earliest version was the BBC production, written by Denis Constanduros and directed by John Glenister, and which screened in 1972. It is in six parts and follows the plot of the novel faithfully. The actors cast as Emma (Doran Godwin) and Mr Knightley (John Carson) were older than in the novel. Doran Godwin was in her thirties and John Carson was forty-five. Nevertheless, they received good critical acclaim. The series was mainly filmed on sets and the outdoor scenes were rather lacking.

In 1996, two versions appeared. One was the film directed and scripted by Douglas McGrath, starring Gwyneth Paltrow and Jeremy Northam, and intended for general release. The other version was a film intended for television release.

The McGrath film enjoyed mainly positive critical reception. It has very pretty leading actors, although Toni Colette is a strange choice for Harriet. She looks too old to be a girl in her late teens and does not have the sweet, artless charm of Austen's character. In the novel, Mr Knightley confesses to Mrs Weston how much he enjoys looking at Emma, and the camera rarely leaves Gwyneth Paltrow, constantly showing her to advantage, in sunlight or candlelight, and against picturesque backgrounds. In fact, the film is visually a treat. Some reviews declared that Paltrow was too attractive to be a credible Emma. In fact, she is a rather soft Emma, without the strong negatives of snobbishness and vanity with which Austen has imbued her in the novel.

The relationship between Emma and Mr Knightley is given prominence, while the parallel relationship between Frank Churchill and Jane Fairfax, crucial to Emma's development, is pushed into the background. Frank Churchill, played by Ewan McGregor, (in a bad wig) is suitably charming and handsome. Mrs Bates is presented as rather doddery and vague, while Miss Bates' garrulity has been moderated.

The 1996 television film of *Emma*, directed by Diarmuid Lawrence, dramatised by Andrew Davies and starring Kate Beckinsale as Emma and Mark Strong as Mr Knightley is quite short and so events seem to be hurried up, sometimes at the expense of meaning. The scenes have been rearranged and this has the effect of rushing along key elements in the plot. All of the early growing influence of Emma over Harriet, the rejected proposal of Robert Martin and Emma's attempts to bring Harriet and Mr Elton together are all rushed through. Thus, we do not develop sufficient sympathy for Emma after Mr Elton's sudden proposal.

Kate Beckinsale received very favourable reviews for this film and was generally agreed to be a very credible Emma. In this version, Mr Knightley is a gloomy figure, who seems to be constantly attempting to educate Emma in a more egalitarian view of the classes. Jane Fairfax is given a much stronger presence in this film than in McGrath's.

The harvest festival scene which has been added at the end of the film is an attempt to show the classes all mingling happily, something of which there is no suggestion at the end of *Emma*. This is part of the film's political subtext, and for many readers of *Emma*, will seem to be an unnecessary and jarring addition.

In 2009, a four-part miniseries, directed by Jim O'Hanlon, scripted by Sandy Welch, and starring Romola Garai as Emma and Johnny Lee Miller as Mr Knightley, was screened. The length allowed greater faithfulness to the novel. This version begins with shots of the three motherless babies — Emma, Jane and Frank. The underlying theme of the series seems to be the search for happiness. Emma is portrayed as good-natured and well-intentioned.

A new film version of *Emma*, directed by Autumn de Wilde, was released in 2020 to good critical reception. It featured Anya Taylor-Joy as a spiky Emma and Johnny Flynn as a fairly young George Knightley. The script, adapted by Eleanor Catton, the Man Booker Prize-winning author, manages to hint at female empowerment and to mildly challenge the social hierarchies of the day. It is a visually lavish production, with real chemistry between the two main characters and a strong supporting cast, notably Miranda Hart as Miss Bates and Bill Nighy as Mr Woodhouse.

As well as these mainstream offerings, there have been other films related in either plot or themes to the original novel. One of these is the 1995 film, *Clueless*, directed by Amy Heckerling and starring Alicia Silverstone and Paul Rudd. This is set in California and follows the theme of hubris leading to regret and greater self-knowledge. Cher, the heroine, is as equally self-deceived as Emma, and undergoes a process of moral improvement. In the film, this improvement is paralleled by a choice of more conservative clothes.

In *Clueless*, use is made of voice-overs by Cher, which emphasise the gap between how matters are and how she perceives them. These have something of the function of the third-person narrator, as they reveal her self-absorption.

Recently, there has been an Indian film, *Aisha*, which loosely follows the events and themes of *Emma*. It is set in Delhi and is just a moderately amusing but basically superficial adaptation.

Emma Approved is a fictional vlog of short (4 to 6 minutes) episodes, and available on the Pemberley Digital website or on YouTube. It is set in Los Angeles, with Emma transmuted into an event planner. Although the characters have different occupations (Mr Elton is a senator), this version follows the plot quite closely.

Critical Reception

Early Critical Reception

Jane Austen's first novels were published anonymously, under the pseudonym of 'a lady', as it was not then regarded as respectable for women to work and receive remuneration. Being a writer would have fallen into the category of work. However, her novels were circulated among the aristocracy and their authorship was an open secret. Austen kept a record of the comments made about her work. There were very few critical reviews and most focused on the suitability of the works for women to read. A more significant review was that of Walter Scott and appeared in the March 1816 "Quarterly Review". He approved of Austen's comic characters, but he also praised her ability to depict ordinary situations and retain the readers' interest. A little later in the "Quarterly Review" of 1861, Richard Whateley recognised Austen's insightful capacity to portray female characters. Julia Cavanagh in English Women of Letters (1862) paid tribute to Austen's keen powers of observation which allowed her to create realistic characters. However, she found Austen's plots fairly dull.

During Victorian times, Austen's novels were eclipsed by the more colourful novels of Charles Dickens. There was still a small dedicated readership of her novels. The publication by Jane Austen's nephew, James Austen Leigh's biography, *A Memoir of Jane Austen* in 1869, hugely increased interest. This coincided with a reissue of her novels in very cheap editions. This allowed greater numbers of people to be introduced to Austen's work over the next years and it also created a disconnection between the 'Janeites', those who saw themselves as an elite truly appreciating the subtleties of the novels, and the new readers.

The Twentieth Century

The first significant critic of the twentieth century was A.C. Bradley. In his 1911 essay, he saw Jane Austen as concerned with presenting both humour and a moral outlook. In contrast, D.W. Harding's 1940 study thought that Austen's humour was too sarcastic. In *The Great Tradition* (1948), a hugely influential study, F.R Leavis praised Austen's melding of realism and satire.

In 1951, Arnold Kettle declared that Austen was limited by her acceptance of the status quo of social class and her failure to see any difficulties caused by class divisions. He also wondered whether Austen's work really resonated with twentieth century readers. (In 1994, Alistair Duckworth presented a completely contrary view about Austen's treatment of class to Kettle. He saw *Emma*, in particular, as raising the growing phenomenon of class consciousness.)

In 1955, Lionel Trilling, another significant twentieth century critic, saw Austen as offering hope in an uncertain world. This idea has been raised by some more recent critics to explain the modern interest in Austen with the proliferation of adaptations and spin-offs, and the rise of the modern 'Janeites'.

Two twentieth century critics who focused on Jane Austen's narrative style were Ian Watt and Wayne Booth. In 1957 in *The Rise of the Novel*, Ian Watt praised her ability to use free indirect discourse, blending subjective and objective viewpoints. In 1961, in *The Rhetoric of Fiction*, Booth identified three points of view in *Emma*: Emma's, Mr Knightley's and the omniscient narrator. Booth was concerned with the way in which Austen retained the reader's interest in and sympathy for the narcissistic heroine.

Much criticism of the later twentieth century examined Austen's overall intentions for her novels. Did she intend to write *bildungsroman* (coming-of-age novels)? Some critics felt that all her novels were about the growth of self-knowledge.

Other critics have debated whether her intention was to write 'marriage stories'. Were the various heroines rewarded for virtue or for personal improvement by making good marriages? Or did Austen bow to what the readers of her day would have expected?

Historicist Criticism

Late twentieth century criticism looked for postcolonial, Marxist and feminist themes in Austen's work. Historicist criticism examines the context within which Austen was writing and looks for evidence of her attitudes to such issues as social divisions, slavery and the revolutionary ideas of the day. Such a study of *Emma* would search for attitudes to the lower classes and perhaps question the manner in which the comfort of the gentry depended on the largely invisible servant class. The limitations on Jane Fairfax by her poverty and the class implications of her marriage to Frank Churchill would merit study.

An influential study was Marilyn Butler's *Jane Austen and the War of Ideas*, which looked at her novels against the political and ideological climate of the day. Butler concluded that Austen was conservative and accepted the patriarchal social system.

Feminist Criticism

Feminist criticism examines the power or lack of power which female characters have, and how much they conform to the traditional social hierarchy or seek to subvert it. Some critics have agreed with Butler that Austen portrayed and accepted female submission to the system. Others have seen Austen as subtly subverting the system. Perhaps, Mr Knightley's move to Hartfield and the upsetting of the normal patriarchal situation in which the woman is absorbed into the man's household, might be seen as evidence of this subversion.

With particular regard to *Emma*, critics have commented on the power enjoyed by Emma, Mrs Elton and Mrs Churchill. This has been seen as evidence of Jane Austen's feminist sentiments. Others have seen Emma's marriage as her capitulation to the social mores and evidence of how little power she actually has. The debate still continues.

Recent Criticism

Incisive and sometimes divisive criticism continues. Some recent critical works examine the phenomenon of the 'Austen Industry' – adaptations, spin-offs, festivals – and the way Austen has been absorbed into modern culture.

Genre

Emma has been seen as belonging to a number of genres: a comedy of manners, a *bildungsroman* or coming-of-age novel, a realistic novel, or a romance.

A comedy of manners satirizes the manners and pretensions of society and questions accepted societal values. The term "Comedy of manners" is more properly applied to plays, e.g. *The Importance of Being Earnest* by Oscar Wilde. The more correct term is "novel of manners". Jane Austen's novels have often been categorised in this way because of their strongly comic elements. However, the concerns of *Emma* go beyond the confines of a novel of manners.

Some critics have classified *Emma* as a *bildungsroman* or coming-of-age novel. Certainly, Emma learns some painful lessons and grows in maturity as a result. Other critics have objected that as Emma is almost twenty-one at the beginning of the novel, she is too old to credibly be the protagonist in a coming-of-age story. *Emma* can be seen as concerned with more than the protagonist's personal growth.

The romance novels of Austen's day focused on emotion and imagination. *Emma*, with its restraint does not really fit easily into this category either.

Jane Austen's talent for realism, for creating authentic characters and recreating ordinary situations, has led to her novels being lumped in with the realistic novels of the day. However, these realistic novels, e.g. *Robinson Crusoe* by Daniel Dafoe were often larger than life in their plots and characters. *Emma* does not fit comfortably here either.

Jane Austen's novels do not fit easily into any of these categories of genre. Perhaps, we can say *Emma* has elements of a novel of manners, enhanced by social realism and similar in construction to the coming-of-age novel. What do you think?

Essay Questions

1. Jane Austen famously said that Emma was a heroine whom 'no one but myself will much like'. How then, does Emma retain our interest and sympathy?
2. In what ways is *Emma* a 'coming of age' story?
3. Discuss the themes of truth and falsity as they are revealed in *Emma*.
4. It has been said that Jane Austen novels are all about marriage and money. Can *Emma* be described in this way?
5. How does *Emma* portray interesting ideas about appearance and reality?
6. Explain how Austen's use of irony illuminates the realities of social class in the world of *Emma*.
7. Despite being written more than two hundred years ago, why does *Emma* continue to resonate with readers?
8. How does *Emma* portray interesting ideas about power?
9. Charlotte Bronte famously said that Austen's writing lacked 'passion'. Is this true of *Emma*?
10. The critic D.W. Harding described Jane Austen's attitude towards society as 'regulated hatred'. Is there evidence of this attitude in *Emma*?
11. Jane Austen's novels have enjoyed a great resurgence of interest in them in modern times. Discuss why this might be so, with particular emphasis on *Emma*.
12. Emma has been described as both the protagonist and the antagonist of the novel, *Emma*. Why might this be so?

Resources

- Marilyn Butler (1975 / 1990) *Jane Austen and the War of Ideas.* Clarenden Press, Oxford.
- Sandra M. Gilbert and Susan Gubar (1979) *The Madwoman in the Attic: The Woman Writer and the Nineteenth Century Literary Imagination.* Yale University Press, New Haven.
- Mona Scheuermann (2012) *Reading Jane Austen.* Palgrave Macmillan, New York.
- Fay Weldon (1984) *Letters to Alice on First Reading Jane Austen.* Coronet, London.
- JASNA — the Jane Austen Society of North America has many excellent articles online. The website is – *www.jasna.org/persuasions/on-line/*
- There is useful information on the characters and plots of Austen's novels on this website — *www.pemberley.com*
- Another website with information on Jane Austen novels is — *www.victorianweb.org*
- Also look at — *www.janeausten.ac.uk*

Glossary

Astley's	The Royal Amphitheatre.
backgammon	A board game.
barouche-landau	A big carriage with four wheels and extra seats.
beaufit	Buffet.
cara sposo	Dear husband. (Should be caro sposo – Mrs Elton has it wrong at times.)
charade	A rhyming riddle popular in Regency times.
chuse	Old fashioned spelling of 'choose'.
cockade	A knot of ribbons on a baby's bonnet.
coxcomb	A silly conceited man too concerned about his appearance. (See also – dandy and fop.)
come-at-able	Within reach, attainable.
court plaister	Sticking plaster made of silk.
dandy	A man too concerned about his appearance.
decorum	Behaviour in keeping with good manners and convention.
deedily	Very earnestly.
espalier	A fruit tree trained on a framework.
fancy-work	Embroidery.
fop	A man too concerned about his appearance.
garters	Stretchy bands used to keep up stockings.
gentility	Social superiority as shown by correct ways of behaving, good manners and appearance.
gruel	A thin porridge.
hazle	An older spelling of 'hazel'.
humourist	Witty.

huswife	Small case for needles and thread.
natural daughter	Daughter born outside marriage.
Pembroke	A small, drop-leaf table.
prosings	Boring, idle chatter.
rout-cakes	Rich cakes.
spencer	A close-fitting jacket.
spruce beer	Beer brewed from the needles of the spruce tree.
stomacher	A decorated triangular panel on the front of a dress.
Swizzerland	Switzerland.
tippet	A small cape.
valetudinarian	A person who worries excessively about their health

Notes

